A
Intro
Su

ALSO AVAILABLE

(by the same author)

A Concise Introduction to SuperCalc5

by
Noel Kantaris

BERNARD BABANI (publishing) LTD.
THE GRAMPIANS
SHEPHERDS BUSH ROAD
LONDON W6 7NF
ENGLAND

PLEASE NOTE

Although every care has been taken with the production of this book to ensure that any projects, designs, modifications and/or programs etc. contained herewith, operate in a correct and safe manner and also that any components specified are normally available in Great Britain, the Publishers and Author do not accept responsibility in any way for the failure, including fault in design, of any project, design, modification or program to work correctly or to cause damage to any other equipment that it may be connected to or used in conjunction with, or in respect of any other damage or injury that may be so caused, nor do the Publishers accept responsibility in any way for the failure to obtain specified components.

Notice is also given that if equipment that is still under warranty is modified in any way or used or connected with home-built equipment then that warranty may be void.

© 1989 BERNARD BABANI (publishing) LTD

First Published — December 1989

British Library Cataloguing in Publication Data:
Kantaris, Noel
    A concise introduction to SuperCalc5
    1. Microcomputer systems. Spreadsheet packages. SuperCalc
    I. Title
    005.36'9

    ISBN 0 85934 219 0

Typeset direct from disc by Commercial Colour Press, London E7.
Printed and Bound in Great Britain by Cox & Wyman Ltd, Reading

ABOUT THIS BOOK

This Concise Introduction to SuperCalc5 was written to help the beginner. The material in the book is presented on the "what you need to know first, appears first" basis, although the underlying structure of the book is such that you don't have to start at the beginning and go right through to the end. The more experienced user can start from any section, as the sections have been designed to be self contained.

SuperCalc5 is an integrated package containing three major types of applications; spreadsheets, graphics and data management. The package is operated by selecting commands from menus or by writing special 'macros' which utilise a Command Language to chain together menu commands. Each method of accessing the package is discussed separately, but the emphasis is mostly in the area of menu-driven command selection.

One of the major enhancements of SuperCalc5 over previous versions of the package and those of other competitors is its ability to work with multipage and multiple spreadsheets on low level existing hardware, such as XT compatibles. Data linking between pages in memory or spreadsheets on disc, allows for three-dimensional work. The ability to link pages should encourage the user to become more structured in his design approach to spreadsheet applications, but at a price.

Since all pages of a spreadsheet must be resident in memory at once, to work in three dimensions, you will require quite a lot more memory that the typical 512 or 640 KBytes of memory available with most PCs. For this very reason, the examples in this book are first discussed and implemented using a flat, one-dimensional, spreadsheet so that those of you who don't have lots of memory can benefit from them. However, since structured design is of prime importance, spreadsheet design layouts are discussed whenever appropriate.

This book was written with the busy person in mind. You don't need to read hundreds of pages to find out the core of a subject, when fewer pages can do the same thing quite adequately! Naturally, selectivity of subject matter is of paramount importance, so the reader does not miss vital points. It is, therefore, hoped that the material presented in this concise book, will allow you to get the most out of your computer, when using SuperCalc5, in terms of efficiency and productivity, and that you will be able to do this in the shortest, most effective and informative way.

ABOUT THE AUTHOR

Graduated in Electrical Engineering at Bristol University and after spending three years in the Electronics Industry in London, took up a Tutorship in Physics at the University of Queensland. Research interests in Ionospheric Physics, lead to the degrees of M.E. in Electronics and Ph.D. in Physics. On return to the UK, he took up a Post-Doctoral Research Fellowship in Radio Physics at the University of Leicester, and in 1973 a Senior Lectureship in Engineering at The Camborne School of Mines, Cornwall, where since 1978 he has also assumed the responsibility of Head of Computing.

TRADEMARKS

ACKNOWLEDGEMENTS

I would like to thank colleagues at the Camborne School of Mines for the helpful tips and suggestions which assisted me in the writing of this book.

CONTENTS

INTRODUCTION

SuperCalc5 is a powerful, versatile, software package which is used by business as well as scientific and engineering users. The program's power lies in its ability to emulate everything that can be done by the use of pencil, paper and a calculator. Thus, it is called an 'electronic spreadsheet' or simply a 'spreadsheet', a name also used to describe this and other similar software products. Its power is derived from the power of the computer it is running in, and the flexibility and accuracy with which it can deal with the solution of the various applications it has been programmed to manage. These can vary from budgeting to forecasting to the solution of scientific and engineering problems.

Computer Associates went to great pains to implement SuperCalc5 on existing hardware so that users of previous versions of SuperCalc do not have to change their computers to run SuperCalc5. The new version of the program will run on an IBM XT compatible (a computer equipped with Intel's 8086 or 8088 processor) and does not specifically require an IBM AT compatible (a computer equipped with Intel's superior 80286 processor). In addition, several of the commands from previous versions of SuperCalc which have been improved and renamed, have been kept hidden so that users can still invoke such parts of the program with commands they are familiar with. Also, users who are familiar with Lotus' 1-2-3 commands, can invoke their familiar 1-2-3 menu by issuing the **/Global 1-2-3** command which allows execution of all the 1-2-3 Version 2.01 commands.

SuperCalc5 incorporates some major enhancements to previous versions of the program or indeed to similar programs available by other competitors. One of these is SuperCalc5's ability to multiple and multipage spreadsheets. Page linking provides a three-dimensional emulation which allows the user to create a spreadsheet with several pages (up to 255, depending on the available memory) and link data in those pages to a consolidation page. All such linked pages can be saved under the same spreadsheet name. Links can also be made to other (up to 255), independent SuperCalc or Lotus 1-2-3 spreadsheets, which can either be in memory or on disc. This latter ability allows reference to very large spreadsheets thus making SuperCalc independent from memory restrictions. However, SuperCalc5 supports the LIM Expanded Memory Standard, permitting the use of up to 32 megabytes of memory. Up to three spreadsheets and spreadsheet pages can be viewed on screen at the same time, provided they are resident in memory.

SuperCalc5's graphics have been enhanced to new heights which rival those of stand alone graphics packages. There are over 100 two- and three-dimensional chart and graph types, including bar, stacked bar, pie, area and polar graphs. Charts and graphs can be grouped, clustered and overlapped. Furthermore, the program allows the production of high-quality slides and transparencies. Presentation quality graphics output and camera-ready documents can be produced with SuperCalc's support of both HP LaserJet and PostScript laser printers. Other features include the capability of incorporating lines, boxes, grids, shading and use of different fonts in both spreadsheets and graphs.

Another SuperCalc5 feature is an integrated debugging and auditing capability which allows large and complex spreadsheets to be audited in a simple and precise manner. Auditing can be used to highlight errors, point out relationships between cells, give an overview of spreadsheet patterns and formulae, and provide a macro development and diagnostic environment which can help in the development of correct macros by allowing line-by-line macro execution, the setting of conditional and unconditional breakpoints, and production of a variety of audit reports.

SuperCalc5 provides support for Scientific and Engineering applications with its incorporation of a large number of appropriate commands and functions, such as solution of linear equations, matrix multiplication and inversion, regression analysis, and choice of alternate curve-fitting algorithms. An add-in software manager allows third-party software to be attached to SuperCalc5 which, amongst others, permits powerful database management functions – including SQL-based systems such as Oracle – to be invoked by simply pressing a key.

It is assumed here that you have followed the instructions accompanying the software, relating to its installation on the hard disc of your computer, or its use from a floppy drive. If your are using an already installed package on hard disc, then it is most likely that the files which make up the complete package will be found in a sub-directory of your computer's hard disc, called **Calc**, and that the actual program can be invoked by typing **Calc** or **SC5** at the root directory's prompt. An appropriately written batch file would then locate the sub-directory in which the program's files reside and load the SuperCalc5 program into memory. Furthermore, it is hoped that you are using Release 5, as with earlier releases some sections of the book, such as those dealing with multipage spreadsheets and multiple spreadsheet linking, will not be strictly relevant to you.

Loading the SuperCalc Program:
If your system is correctly implemented on the hard disc, typing **Calc** or **SC5** at the root directory's prompt followed by 'Enter', causes the Computer Associates's logo and SuperCalc5's copyright page to be displayed with the following information at the bottom of the screen:

```
Press F1 for information about SuperCalc or other Computer Associates products
Press any key to start. _
```

On a floppy disc system, you will be prompted to insert the second SuperCalc disc (Product 2) in the A: drive. Pressing 'Enter' displays a blank spreadsheet with the border:

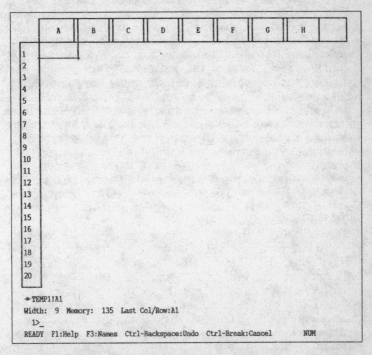

```
→ TEMP1!A1
Width:  9  Memory:  135  Last Col/Row:A1
  1>_
READY  F1:Help  F3:Names  Ctrl-Backspace:Undo  Ctrl-Break:Cancel        NUM
```

Note the last four lines of the display which form the dialogue panel. The four lines are known as the 'Status', 'Prompt', 'Entry' and 'Help' lines, respectively.

3

SuperCalc has just set up a huge electronic page, or spreadsheet, in your computer's memory, many times larger than the small part shown on the screen. Navigation around the spreadsheet is achieved by use of the four arrow cursor keys. Each time one of these keys is pressed, the highlighted bar moves one position right, down, left or up, depending on which arrow key was pressed. Pressing the 'Enter' key also moves the highlighted bar, but in the direction shown by the small arrow appearing in the leftmost position of the 'Status' line. The direction of the arrow changes according to which arrow key was last pressed. The 'PgDn' and 'PgUp' keys can also be used to move vertically 20 rows at a time, while the **Ctrl-Right Arrow**, or **Ctrl-Left Arrow** can be used to move right or left one screen-full at a time. A spreadsheet can be thought of as a two-dimensional table made up of rows and columns. The point where a row and column intersect is called a cell.

When you have finished navigating around the spreadsheet, press the 'Home' key which will bring you to the Home cell, (A1), which is the top left-hand corner of the spreadsheet. This is known as the Home position. Individual cells are identified by column and row location (in that order), with present size extending to 255 columns and 9,999 rows. The columns are labeled from A to Z, followed by AA to AZ, BA to BZ, and so on, to IU, while the rows are numbered from 1 to 9999. The reference points of a cell are known as the cell address. Note that there are several areas on your screen; the displayed area within which you can move the highlighted bar is referred to as the working area of the spreadsheet, while the letters and numbers in the highlighted border around the displayed portion of the spreadsheet form the reference points. It is worth noting that the highlighted bar cannot be moved into this border areas of the spreadsheet.

The location of the highlighted bar is constantly monitored by the 'cell indicator' which is to be found on the left part of the 'Status' line immediately following the 'cursor direction indicator' and the spreadsheet name. As the highlighted bar moves, this indicator displays the address of the cell. The contents of a cell are displayed on the rightmost part of the 'Status line' following the 'cell entry format options indicator', 'protection indicator' and 'data type indicator'. Finally, on the leftmost position of the 'Help' line, the word 'READY' is displayed which indicates the current mode of the program. For a full list of all other indicators, refer to Appendix A.

The GOTO Command:

Sometimes it is necessary to move to a specific address in the spreadsheet which, however, is too far from our present position that using the arrow keys might take far too long to get there. To this end, SuperCalc has implemented the **F5** function key as a 'go to' command. For example, to jump to position HZ5000, press the **F5** key, which will cause SuperCalc to ask for the address of the cell to which it is to jump to. This request appears on the 'Prompt line' of the dialogue panel, on a position immediately below the file name on the 'Status line'. The default address is the address of the highlighted bar.

Now, typing HZ5000 – which is reflected on the 'Entry line' – and pressing 'Enter', causes the highlighted bar to jump to that cell address. To specify a cell address you must always key one or two letters followed by a number. The letters can range from A to IU corresponding to a column, while the numbers can range from 1 to 9999 corresponding to a row. These values are valid provided your system has enough memory to accommodate the maximum size of a spreadsheet. However, do note that unless your computer has 640KB of conventional memory and 384KB of EMS memory, then you cannot hold a spreadsheet of IU columns by 9,999 rows. In fact, the largest spreadsheet that can be held in a 640KB conventional memory is DW columns by 2,000 rows, therefore the above request to jump to location HZ5000 will cause a 'Range Error' to be displayed on the far right of the 'Status line'. To clear the error, press the 'Esc' key once; the 'Esc' key can also be used to cancel a command and escape from a situation before an error occurs. To return to the Home (A1) position, press the 'Home' key.

Entering Information in a Spreadsheet:

We will now investigate how information can be entered into the spreadsheet. But first, return to the Home (A1) position by pressing the 'Home' key, then type in the information given below. As you type, the characters appear in the 'Entry line' of the dialogue panel. Type the words:

PROJECT ANALYSIS

If you make a mistake, press the 'BkSp' key to erase the previous letter or the 'Esc' key to start again. When you have finished, press 'Enter'. Note that what you have just typed in has been entered in cell A1, even though part of the word ANALYSIS appears to be in cell B1. If you use the **Left Arrow** key to highlight cell A1, the words

Text="PROJECT ANALYSIS

appear on the middle of the 'Status line', the string 'Text=' indicating the data type.

Thus, typing any letter at the beginning of a cell results in 'labels' to be formed which are automatically preceded with the double quotes (") character. Pressing 'Enter' inserts the information as a 'label' into the highlighted cell. If the length of a label is longer than the width of a cell, it will continue into the next contiguous cell. If you make any mistakes after pressing the 'Enter' key, you can 'undo' them by pressing **Ctrl-BkSp** which activates the **Undo** facility, restoring into a cell what you had in it before the last entry. If you press **Ctrl-BkSp** twice while the A1 cell is highlighted, the contents of the cell will be blanked with the first press of the key combination, and restored back to your last entry with that of the second.

Now use the arrow keys to move the highlighted bar to cell B3 and type

Jan

and press the Right-Arrow key which will automatically enter the typed information into the cell and also move the highlighted bar to the next cell (C3). Now type

Feb

and again press the Right-Arrow key.
Now move to cell A4 and type

'=

and press 'Enter'.

Note that typing the apostrophe (') and then following it with one or more characters it replicates the entry and fills all empty cells to the right of the highlighted cell with the repeated character(s). The 'data' type indicator, when the cell in which such an entry was made is highlighted, changes to "Rtxt" which stands for 'Repeated text'. To restrict the length of such a repeated entry to say, the range A4:B4, move the highlighted bar to C4 and type an apostrophe (') followed by 'Enter'.

The 'data' type indicator can assume four possible values, as follows:

Ctrl=	Control text (non-printing text, preceded by ǀ)
Form=	Formula entry (formulae or numbers)
Rtxt=	Repeating text
Text=	String text (labels and words)

Finally, move to cell A5 and type

```
Consult:
```

then enter the numbers 14000 and 15000 in cells B5 and C5, respectively.

What you should have on your screen now is the following:

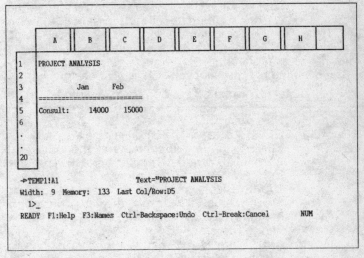

Note how the labels 'Jan' and 'Feb' do not appear above the numbers 14000 and 15000. This is because by default, labels are left justified, while numbers are right justified.

The EDIT Command:
One way of correcting the looks of this spreadsheet is to also right justified the labels 'Jan' and 'Feb' within their respective cells. To do this, move the highlighted bar to cell B3 and press the F2 function key which will allow you to edit the contents of the cell. The cursor is now moved into the 'Entry line' of the dialogue panel. What you see is:

```
5>"Jan
```

with the cursor at the end of the label.

The number preceding the > indicates the current position (in characters) of the cursor. Press the 'Home' key to move the cursor under the quotes (") character, press the 'Ins' key to toggle into insertion mode, and type a left bracket '(' delete it with the 'Del' key. Then press the 'End' key to move the cursor to the end of the string and type full quotes followed by a right bracket '")'. The intended cell contends should now be as follows:

`8>("Jan")`

On pressing the 'Enter' key, the label is now right justified within its cell.

Thus, in general, to edit information already in a cell, move the highlighted bar to the appropriate cell and press the **F2** function key. The cursor keys, the 'Home' and 'End' keys, as well as the 'Ins' and 'Del' keys can be used to move the cursor and/or edit information as required.

The meaning of other function keys is given below:

Table 1. Function Keys and their Meaning

Key	Description
F1	**HELP:** Accesses the HELP screens
F2	**EDIT:** Calls up cell contents to the entry line from READY mode; Toggles on/off EDIT mode from ENTRY or POINT modes
F3	**NAME:** Displays the file directory on Load or Save menus. In **/View** it displays the graph names and in other modes, displays the Name Range Directory
F4	**ABS:** Toggles between the four variations in absolute references in ENTRY mode. In the file directory, **F4** makes the current directory setting the default
F5	**GOTO:** Moves the highlighted bar to a specified cell location
F6	**WINDOW:** Toggles between windows on the spreadsheet
F7	**TLABELS:** Toggles between name and reference display in formulae
F8	**MACRO:** Resumes macro execution
F9	**CALC:** Causes the spreadsheet to calculate or, in ENTRY mode, the entry formula to be solved
F10	**VIEW:** Allows viewing of the currently selected graph

The use of the above function keys will be discussed as and when needed. But it is worth noting that should you need help, at any stage, pressing the function key **F1** will produce the required effect. The first help screen, when the mode indicator is on 'READY', offers help on the following items:

```
Help Index                                           SuperCalc AnswerScreen

  SuperCalc Basics:        Entering Data:            Spreadsheet Format:
  SuperCalc Startup        Erasing Data              Text Display
  Program Defaults         Undo Feature              Number Display
  Optimizing SuperCalc     Hiding Data               Data and Time Display
  Modes and Indicators     Using Point Mode          Currency Format
  Searching for Files      Reference Syntax          Column Width
  Optimizing Memory


  Creating Reports:        Formulas:                 Advanced Topics:
  Printing Reports         Functions                 Macros
  Fonts, Borders & Shade   Cell Reference            Charting
  Creating Lines           Operators                 Using a Database
  Device Selection         Formula Display           How to Parse Data



  Multiple Spreadsheets:   Miscellaneous:            Keys:
  Basic Concepts           Transpose Rows to Columns Keys and Function Keys
  Creating                 Named Ranges              International Keys
  Display Windows          1-2-3 to SuperCalc        Entering ASCII Chars



 RELATED TOPICS:    Slash Commands        // Commands
 ESC=Return to SuperCalc   F2 = How to use Help    F3 = Help Index
```

The above are menu options and can be selected by moving the highlighted bar to the required choice and pressing the 'Enter' key. There is an extensive list of sub-menus under each menu choice. Furthermore, the help command is context sensitive which means that pressing the **F1** function key while in the middle of entering another command, brings up the help screens relevant to the command being entered. This context sensitive help screen might have a choice of items on which help is available.

9

Saving a Spreadsheet:

Now, let us assume that we would like to stop at this point, but would like to save the work entered so far, before leaving the program. First, let us return to the Home position by pressing the 'Home' key. Then we need to use the menu system provided by SuperCalc. Menus are called up with the front slash key (/) which is found on the query (?) key. The forward slash (/) must not be confused with the back slash (\).

On pressing /, a horizontal menu in 'SuperCalc' style appears on the first two lines of the dialogue panel of the screen, as follows:

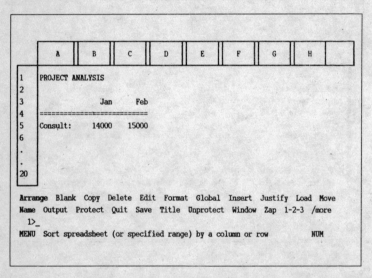

As a menu is a list of options, the first line of the menu lists the options available. The second line describes the option that is currently highlighted by the bar. The highlighted bar on the menu can be moved by pressing the right or left arrow key, the 'Home' and 'Del' key or the Spacebar. Note that the 'mode indicator' at the bottom left-hand corner of the screen now reads 'MENU'.

To make a menu selection, say **S** (for Save), we can either move the highlighted bar down one and four right over the fifth option and press 'Enter', or simply press the first letter of the desired option (**S** in this case). We shall use this last method to select 'Save' – indeed, from now on, we will always use the first letter method as it is quicker. If you make a mistake, simply

10

press the 'Esc' key twice and try again. On selection of 'Save',
the mode option indicator on the bottom left-hand corner of the
screen changes to 'FILE' and we are presented on the 'Entry line'
of the dialogue panel with the command, followed by the drive,
directory and name of the current file to be saved, as follows:

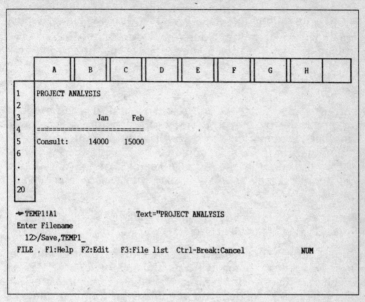

```
        A       B       C       D       E       F       G       H

1   PROJECT ANALYSIS
2
3               Jan     Feb
4   ============================
5   Consult:    14000   15000
6
.
.
20

 ➡ TEMP1!A1                    Text="PROJECT ANALYSIS
  Enter Filename
   12>/Save,TEMP1_
  FILE . F1:Help  F2:Edit   F3:File list  Ctrl-Break:Cancel          NUM
```

The 'Entry line' of the dialogue panel now gives you the
default sub-directory to which data files will be saved. This, in
the case of a hard disc system, should be preferably the

C:\CALC\DATA

sub-directory. Pressing **F3**, produces a list of files on the 'data'
directory. The *.CAL in the boxed section of the screen, indicates
the type of files listed in the lines below. These could be
FILE1.CAL and FILE2.CAL which perhaps contain someone
else's work. If you are the first person to be using the package, it
is more likely that there will not be any filenames of previously
saved work.

If this is not the case with the data path, and you still want to
save your files on your hard disc, it is imperative to change the
default data file path (see next section), so as to save the files
you create into a separate directory from that in which
SuperCalc program files are kept.

To save the present contents of memory to a file you must either accept the existing filename, used to load a previously saved work, or type a new filename. If you choose to save your work under the existing filename, you will be asked whether you would like to **Overwrite** the contents of the file on disc by the contents of the current memory. If you do, type O to confirm you decision. If, on the other hand, you choose to save your work under a new filename, or a different filename from the one used to load it in the first place, then simply type the new name. To end this session, type

PROJECT1

and press the 'Enter' key. The extension .CAL will be added automatically by the program, but not before being asked whether you would like to save **All** of the current work.

Summarizing:- To save spreadsheet files do the following: First, make sure that the mode indicator is on 'READY'. If not, press the 'Esc' key as many times as necessary to achieve it, then

Press /   to reveal the menu options
Press **S**   to select **Save**.

SuperCalc asks for a filename to save under. If this spreadsheet is a newly created one, it will have the default name TEMP1, in which case just type the new name. If the spreadsheet is an old one which was loaded and modified, the original name is offered as the default name to save under. Pressing 'Enter', requires **Overwrite** confirmation. In either case, you will also be asked to confirm that you would like to save **All** of the current work.

Changing the Default Data Drive/Path:
Assuming you want to change the default drive/path to which your data is to be saved, do the following: First, make sure that the mode indicator is on 'READY'. If not, press the 'Esc' key as many times as necessary to achieve it, then

Press /   to reveal the menu options
Press /   to reveal the **more** advanced options
Press **F**   to select **File**
Press **D**   to select **Directory**.

On the 'Entry line', the current directory for data is displayed. To change this, to say the A: drive, type A:.

If, on the other hand, you wanted to save your work on the C:drive, then provided a \DATA sub-directory to the main CALC directory already exists, then type C:\CALC\DATA.

If you want to make this change permanent, then

Press **/**	to reveal the menu options
Press **G**	to select **Global**
Press **K**	to select **Keep**
Press **Y**	for 'Yes', to confirm command.

From now on data will be saved and retrieved from the newly named default drive:\path.

Erasing a Spreadsheet:

To erase a spreadsheet from memory (make sure you have saved your work first), which also clears the screen, do the following:

Press **/**	to reveal the menu options
Press **Z**	to select **Zap**
Press **Y**	for 'Yes', to confirm command.

Your work will disappear. If you didn't mean it, press **Ctrl-BkSp** to 'Undo' the deletion. Always use this command to clear memory and screen of unwanted information before starting with a new spreadsheet. Never switch off your computer in order to clear its memory of unwanted work! Computers are best left running for the entire working period, as switching them on and off too many times in a day can cause hardware failure.

The **/Zap** command offers you, through its sub-menu, the opportunity to **Save** a modified spreadsheet before clearing the computer's memory, or to only clear one specified page from memory rather than the whole spreadsheet.

Loading a Spreadsheet:

An already saved spreadsheet – a spreadsheet file – can be loaded by doing the following:

Press **/**	to reveal the menu options
Press **L**	to select **Load**

SuperCalc asks for a filename to load, with the default file given as TEMP1. Pressing 'Enter', lists the files on the default drive/directory. Use the cursor keys to highlight the required file and press 'Enter' which causes the program to ask you whether you would like the chosen file to **Replace** the existing file in memory. Press 'Enter', if you do.

13

SuperCalc provides a facility whereby files can be consolidated (merged). This facility is part of the Load sub-menu.

Quitting the SuperCalc Program:
To quit the program, press the forward slash (/) to display the menus. Make sure that this is done when the mode indicator is on 'READY'. If it is not, press the 'Esc' key as many times as it is necessary for the mode indicator to change to 'READY'. Then press the forward slash (/) key to display the menus and press Q (for Quit).

Before quitting, SuperCalc prompts you again, because if you quit a session without saving your spreadsheet you will lose any changes made. The prompt is of the form

```
No   Yes To Save DOS
  7>/Quit,_
MENU  Do not exit SuperCalc — return to spreadsheet
```

with the highlighted bar over the 'No'. Pressing Y (for Yes) ends the SuperCalc session and the program returns either to the DOS operating system or whatever menu was used, in the first place, to load SuperCalc.

FILLING IN A SPREADSHEET

We will use, as an example on how a spreadsheet can be built up, the few entries on 'Project Analysis' which we used in the Introduction to SuperCalc. If you haven't saved the PROJECT1 example, don't worry as you could just as easily start afresh. If you have saved PROJECT1, then enter the SuperCalc program, and at the 'READY' mode, type

Press /   to reveal the menu options
Press L   to select **Load**

or in abbreviated form, **/Load,** which is the format that will be used throughout the rest of this book. SuperCalc will ask you the name of the file to load. Press the 'Enter' key which will cause the program to display the message

File not on specified drive or directory

on the screen, but also list the files on the default drive/directory. Use the cursor keys to highlight PROJECT1 and press 'Enter' to load the required file. The program will ask you whether you would like to **Replace** the current contents of memory with the contents of the selected filename. Confirmation causes the chosen spreadsheet to be displayed on screen.

Now use the **F2** function key to 'Edit' existing entries or simply retype the contents of cells (see below) so that you end up with the spreadsheet shown on the next page.

Formatting Labels:
Labels can be formatted with the help of the following prefixes:

"	to left justify a string
("	to right justify a string. It also requires the closing characters ") after the string
'	to repeat a character. It also requires the character ' to be typed into the first cell to the right of the range of cells in which repeated characters are wanted, so as to end repetition.

With these in mind, the information in cell A1 (PROJECT ANALYSIS: ADEPT CONSULTANTS LTD) was entered left justified. In fact we just typed in the label in A1 without preceding it with the double quotes as this is the default entry mode for labels. Similarly, all the labels appearing in column A were just typed in, as shown.

15

The labels relating to the months in cells B3, C3, D3 and E3 were entered with the characters (" prefixing them and ") following them, so as to right justify them within their respective cell.

Repeated information, like the double line stretching from A4 to E4 was entered by first highlighting cell A4 and typing

' =

On pressing 'Enter' the equal character (=) sign fills all empty cells to the right of the highlighted cell. To restrict the length of such a repeated entry to the range A4:E4, move the highlighted bar to F4 and type an apostrophe (') and press 'Enter'.

	A	B	C	D	E	F	G	H	
1	PROJECT ANALYSIS: ADEPT CONSULTANTS LTD								
2									
3		Jan	Feb	Mar	1st Qrt				
4	==								
5	Consult:	14000	15000	16000					
6	==								
7	Costs:								
8	Wages	2000	3000	4000					
9	Travel	400	500	600					
10	Rent	300	300	300					
11	Heat/Lght	150	200	150					
12	Phone/Fax	250	300	350					
13	Adverts	1100	1200	1300					
14	--								
15	Tot Cost:								
16	==								
17	Profit:								
18	==								
19	Cumulat:								
20	==								

✦PROJECT1!A1   Text="PROJECT ANALYSIS: ADEPT CONSULTANTS LTD
Width: 9 Memory: 132 Last Col/Row:F20
   1>_
READY F1:Help F3:Names Ctrl-Backspace:Undo Ctrl-Break:Cancel   NUM

Entering Text, Numbers and Formulae:
When text, numbers or formulae are entered into a cell, or reference is made to the contents of a cell by the cell address, or a SuperCalc function is entered into a cell, then the mode indicator changes from 'READY' to 'ENTRY'.

Returning to our example of PROJECT ANALYSIS, move the highlighted bar to B5 and start entering the 'consultancy' income of the company. As soon as the first number is typed into the line below the cell indicator (the number 1 of the 14000), the mode indicator changes to 'ENTRY' and when the complete amount is typed in, pressing 'Enter' inserts it into the specified cell, right justifying the number within the cell width. Now complete typing in the rest of the amounts into cells C5 and D5.

We can find the 1st quarter total income from consultancy, by highlighting cell E5 and typing

```
B5+C5+D5
```

and on pressing 'Enter' the total first quarter consultancy income is added from the above formula and the result placed into E5.

Now complete the insertion into the spreadsheet of the various amounts under 'costs' and then save the result into the file

```
PROJECT2
```

before going on any further. Remember that saving your work on disc often enough is a good thing to get used to, as even the shortest power cut can cause the loss of hours of hard work!

Entering Functions:
In our example, writing a formula that adds the contents of three columns is not too difficult or lengthy task. But imagine having to add 20 columns! For this reason SuperCalc has an in-built summation function (for others see Appendix B) in the form of

```
SUM( )
```

which can be used to add any number of columns (or rows).

To illustrate how this function can be used, move the highlighted bar to E5 and type

```
SUM(
```
          which changes the mode indicator to 'ENTRY'

17

then use the arrow keys to move the cell pointer (note that pressing an arrow key changes the mode indicator to 'POINT') to the start of the summation range (B5 in this case), then press . (period) to anchor the starting point of range, and use the arrow keys to move the cell pointer to the end of the summation range (in this case D5). What appears against the cell indicator is the entry

```
SUM(B5:D5
```

which has to be completed by typing the closing bracket and pressing 'Enter'. The first few lines on your screen should look as follows:

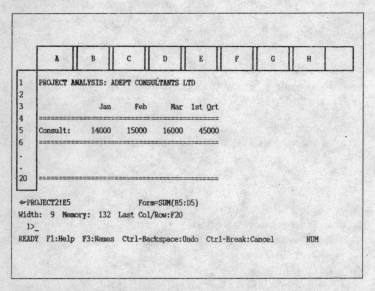

```
        A        B        C        D        E      F      G      H
1    PROJECT ANALYSIS: ADEPT CONSULTANTS LTD
2
3                 Jan      Feb      Mar  1st Qrt
4    ==================================================
5    Consult:   14000    15000    16000    45000
6    ==================================================
.
.
20   ==================================================

→PROJECT2!E5                Form=SUM(B5:D5)
Width:  9  Memory:  132  Last Col/Row:F20
  1>_
READY  F1:Help  F3:Names  Ctrl-Backspace:Undo  Ctrl-Break:Cancel        NUM
```

The /Copy Command:
To replicate information into other cells we could repeat the above procedure (in this particular case entering the SUM() function in each cell within the cell range E8 through E13), or we could use the /C (for Copy) command which is by far the quickest method of copying information from one cell to a range of other cells. This command is not restricted to functions, but can also be used equally well to copy text, numbers, or formulae.

To copy the function in cell E5 into the target range E8 through E13, ensure that you are in the 'READY' mode (press 'Esc' until you are), then move the cell pointer to E5, and press **/Copy**.

18

At this point, you'll be asked for the range to copy from. In this case, the cell pointer (note that the mode indicator has changed to 'POINT') is at the cell we want to start copying from and the entire copy range is highlighted (i.e. the range is given by E5 to E5), therefore press

Enter	to confirm the range

which will cause SuperCalc to ask you to enter the range to copy to. Now press

Down Arrow	to move to the starting location of the range
.	(period) to anchor the first target cell
Down Arrow	to select and highlight the target cell range
Enter	to confirm the target range.

Immediately this command is confirmed, its execution causes the actual sums of the 'relative' columns to appear on the target area. Notice that when the highlighted bar is on E5 the function target range is B5:D5, while when the highlighted bar is moved to E8 the function target range changes to B8:D8 which indicates that copying formulae with this method causes the 'relative' target range to be copied. Had the 'absolute' target range been copied instead, the result of the various summations would have been wrong.

Now complete the insertion of functions and formulae in the rest of the spreadsheet, noting that 'Total Cost' is the summation of rows 8 through 13, 'Profit' is the subtraction of 'Total Cost' from 'Consultancy', and that 'Cumulat' in row 19 refers to cumulative profit.

If you make any mistakes and copy information into cells you did not mean to, then use the /B (for Blank) command.

The /Blank Command:
To blank the contents within a range of adjacent cells, highlight the first cell and press /Blank, then press the Right, Left, Up or Down arrow key a number of times to highlight the row or column range to blank, and press 'Enter' to confirm the selected range.

To blank a block of cells, highlight one corner cell of the block and press /Blank, then press

.	(period) to anchor the first corner of the block
Arrows	to complete highlighting the block of target cells
Enter	to confirm the block selection.

19

Now add another column to your spreadsheet to calculate (and place in column F) the average monthly values of earnings, costs, and profit, using the AVG( ) function.

The spreadsheet, up to this point, should look as follows:

	A	B	C	D	E	F	G	H	
1	PROJECT ANALYSIS: ADEPT CONSULTANTS LTD								
2									
3		Jan	Feb	Mar	1st Qrt	Average			
4	===								
5	Consult:	14000	15000	16000	45000	15000			
6	===								
7	Costs:								
8	Wages	2000	3000	4000	9000	3000			
9	Travel	400	500	600	1500	500			
10	Rent	300	300	300	900	300			
11	Heat/Lght	150	200	150	500	166.6667			
12	Phone/Fax	250	300	350	900	300			
13	Adverts	1100	1200	1300	3600	1200			
14	---								
15	Tot Cost:	4200	5500	6700	16400	5466.667			
16	===								
17	Profit:	9800	9500	9300	28600	9533.333			
18	===								
19	Cumulat:	9800	19300	28600					
20	===								

```
➔ PROJECT2!F5              Form=AVG(B5:D5)
Width: 9  Memory: 131  Last Col/Row:G20
  1>_
READY  F1:Help  F3:Names  Ctrl-Backspace:Undo  Ctrl-Break:Cancel        NUM
```

Formatting Numbers:

Note the contents of F11, F15 and F17, under the 'Average' column, are no longer whole numbers. Furthermore, the number of digits after the decimal point is variable and depends on the available space – the width of the appropriate field.

To make our present spreadsheet more presentable, we need to format specific cells so that we are in control of what is printed out. To format the contents of a numeric cell or block of cells, highlight the starting target cell (in our example, F5) and press **/Format Column**, at which point you'll be asked to enter the range.

20

If the highlighted bar is on the first cell of the range, press

.	(period) to anchor the beginning of the range
Down Arrow	to highlight range F5:F20
Enter	which causes SuperCalc to reveal another menu.

Now, press $ to select currency-type of format (xx.xx), and press

| Enter | to accept the selection. |

Numbers will now be displayed in currency format but with the $ sign prefixing them (to change this, see below).

   It is possible that when numbers are formatted in this way, they might not fit into the default allocated space (width) of given cells. If that happens, you will know it as SuperCalc fills such cells with the 'great than' (>) sign.

Changing the Default Width of Cells:
To change the width of columns (in order to accommodate either large numbers or numbers expressed in the form of currency, press **/Format Column** and press

.	(period) to anchor beginning of target range
Arrows	to highlight the target area
Enter	to confirm selection.

At this point, another menu appears on the last line of the dialogue panel. Now, select **Width** which will display the current width of the columns in the selected target area. At this point, type in the new width and press 'Enter' to confirm choice.

   It is suggested to use the above commands to change the widths of columns B through E from the default value of 9 to 11, and that of column F to 12. This will be necessary as soon as you attempt to prefix the numbers in these cells with a currency symbol.

   When the spreadsheet is 'Saved', this column width display format will be saved with it.

Changing Default Currency & Date Formats:
To change the default formats of currency and from $ to UK's £, use the **/Global Optimum Present Before Enter** command, and type

£	for the new prefix character
Enter	to confirm choice
q	To return to READY mode.

To change the default format for date from MM-DD-YY to UK's DD.MM.YY, use the **/Format User-defined Date** command, which accesses the User-defined Date Format menu, and type

8	to select the eighth date option
A	to select **Accept**.

To make these options permanent for use as default values in this and all future spreadsheets, make sure you are in the READY mode, and then use the **/Global Keep** command.

Creating Output Reports:
A spreadsheet can be transformed into a printed output with the help of the **/Output** and **/Global** commands. Computer Associates have added features into SuperCalc5 which use the superior enhancement printing capabilities of two laser printers; the HP LaserJet and the PostScript standard. Other features include the capability of incorporating lines, boxes, grids, shading and use of different fonts in both spreadsheet and graph outputs.

However, before you can use the features of the **/Output** command, you must first tell SuperCalc which device you are using as your text reports and/or as your graphics reports, so as to get the best possible output results.

To do this, first use the **/Global Spreadsheet Device** command, which will offer you a choice between B&W and Colour printers. Choosing one of these options reveals a menu of printer manufactures, with a further sub-menu of supported printers once a specific manufacturer has been chosen. Then use the **/Global Graphics Device** command to similarly specify your output device for graphics.

To make these selections the default permanent options, make sure you are in the READY mode, and then use the **/Global Keep** command.

Printing a Spreadsheet:
To print a spreadsheet, make sure that the printer is switched on and that the highlighted bar is in the 'Home' position and the spreadsheet mode is on 'READY'. Then use the **/Output Printer Range** command, and press

.	(period) to anchor range from Home – cell A1
Arrows	to move cell pointer to the bottom right-hand corner of the rectangle you wish to print
Enter	to confirm selection
A	to select **Align** which resets the line counter to zero, to begin a new page
G	to select **Go** and send the report to the printer.

It is, of course, assumed that you have configured your system to your printer. If you have not done this configuration, your printer might not respond to your print commands. On completion of the printout, press

Q	to select **Quit**

and return to the 'READY' mode.

A request to print again, will automatically remember the previous range. If you require a different range, then when the highlighted rectangular area appears on screen, as a result of previous print commands, cancel the current range by pressing the 'Esc' key, then move the cell pointer to the required starting position (top left-hand corner) of target area, and press

.	(period) to anchor top left hand corner of rectangle
Arrows	to move the cell pointer to the bottom right-hand corner of rectangle you require to print
Enter	to confirm selection

If your spreadsheet is too wide for the default 'portrait' option settings, you could use the **/Output Printer Options Layout Orientation** command and choose the **Landscape** mode.

For the moment, carry out the suggested formatting changes to column F of spreadsheet PROJECT2 and then arrange for the £ sign to prefix the consultancy entries in row 5. You will have to have changed the default 'Currency' format of your spreadsheet in order to do this successfully. These formatting changes to row 5, as well as column ranges F8:F13, F15 and F17 are best executed by using the **/Format Entry** command, then type

B5:F5	to select the range to format
U	to select **User-defined** option
N	to select **Number**
3	to select the 3rd type of number display
'Enter'	to **Accept** selection.

Now, save the resultant spreadsheet as PROJECT3 and use your printer to print out the rectangle A1 to F20. Your printout should look as follows:

```
        A          B          C          D          E          F          G

1   PROJECT ANALYSIS: ADEPT CONSULTANTS LTD
2
3                  Jan        Feb        Mar     1st Qrt    Average
4   ==============================================================================
5   Consult:  £14,000.00 £15,000.00 £16,000.00 £45,000.00 £15,000.00
6   ==============================================================================
7   Costs:
8   Wages         2000       3000       4000       9000  £3,000.00
9   Travel         400        500        600       1500    £500.00
10  Rent           300        300        300        900    £300.00
11  Heat/Lght      150        200        150        500    £166.67
12  Phone/Fax      250        300        350        900    £300.00
13  Adverts       1100       1200       1300       3600  £1,200.00
14  ------------------------------------------------------------------------------
15  Tot Cost:     4200       5500       6700      16400  £5,466.67
16  ==============================================================================
17  Profit:       9800       9500       9300      28600  £9,533.33
18  ==============================================================================
19  Cumulat:      9800      19300      28600
20  ==============================================================================

➡ PROJECT3!F5           U3    Form=AVG(B5:D5)
Width: 12  Memory: 131  Last Col/Row:G20
  1>_
READY  F1:Help  F3:Names  Ctrl-Backspace:Undo  Ctrl-Break:Cancel        NUM
```

ADDING SPREADSHEET SKILLS

We will now use the spreadsheet saved under PROJECT3 (see end of previous chapter) to show how we can add to it, rearrange information in it and freeze titles in order to make entries easier, before going on to discuss more advanced topics. If you haven't saved PROJECT3 on disc, it will be necessary for you to enter the information shown below into SuperCalc, so that you can benefit from what is to be introduced at this point. Having done this, do save your work under PROJECT3 before going on with the suggested alterations.

If you have saved PROJECT3, then enter SuperCalc and when the mode indicator reads 'READY', type **/Load** and press 'Enter'. This will list the files on the default drive, from which select PROJECT3 by highlighting it and pressing 'Enter'. You will now be asked whether you would like this file to **Replace** what is in memory. On pressing 'Enter', the spreadsheet is displayed on the screen as shown below.

	A	B	C	D	E	F	G
1	PROJECT ANALYSIS: ADEPT CONSULTANTS LTD						
2							
3		Jan	Feb	Mar	1st Qrt	Average	
4	===						
5	Consult:	£14,000.00	£15,000.00	£16,000.00	£45,000.00	£15,000.00	
6	===						
7	Costs:						
8	Wages	2000	3000	4000	9000	£3,000.00	
9	Travel	400	500	600	1500	£500.00	
10	Rent	300	300	300	900	£300.00	
11	Heat/Lght	150	200	150	500	£166.67	
12	Phone/Fax	250	300	350	900	£300.00	
13	Adverts	1100	1200	1300	3600	£1,200.00	
14	---						
15	Tot Cost:	4200	5500	6700	16400	£5,466.67	
16	===						
17	Profit:	9800	9500	9300	28600	£9,533.33	
18	===						
19	Cumulat:	9800	19300	28600			
20	===						

```
→ PROJECT3!F5        U3    Form=AVG(B5:D5)
Width: 12  Memory: 131  Last Col/Row:G20
  1>_
READY  F1:Help  F3:Names  Ctrl-Backspace:Undo  Ctrl-Break:Cancel        NUM
```

What we would like to do now is to add some more information to the spreadsheet with the insertion of another quarter's figures in columns between E and F.

The /Insert Command:
To insert columns (or rows) into a spreadsheet, move the highlighted bar to the column (or row) where insertion is to be made (in this case we want to insert columns, therefore position the highlighted bar on F1) and type **/Insert Column** (or **Row,** if inserting rows), which asks for the range to insert. At this point, and if the highlighted bar is on the cell where insertion is to be made, press

.	(period) to anchor the beginning of column (F1 in this case)
Right arrow	to highlight range F1:I1
Enter	to confirm range selection and execute.

On execution, empty cells are inserted into the spreadsheet in the requested range, and in this case, the column headed 'Average' now appears in column J.

We could now start entering information into the empty columns, but if we did this first, we would then have to first replicate and then edit appropriately the various formulae used to calculate the various results for the first quarter.

An alternative way is to copy everything from the first quarter to the second and then only edit the actual numeric information within the various columns. We will choose this second method to achieve our goal. First highlight cell B3 and then type **/Copy** which asks for range to be copied. Now use

Right arrow	to highlight columns B3:E3
.	(period) to anchor top right-hand corner of rectangle
Down arrow	to highlight block of rows 3 to 20
Enter	to confirm selection
Right arrow	to highlight cell F3
Enter	to confirm selection and execute.

Note that cells F5:I5 contain a string made up of 'greater than' (>) characters indicating that the width of the inserted cells is insufficient to hold the numeric information allotted to them in the chosen format. It will, therefore, be necessary to change the default width of the corresponding columns from 9 to 11 characters. Do this with the command **/Format Column** and then press

.	(period) to anchor beginning of target range
Arrows	to highlight the target area
Enter	to confirm selection.

At this point, select **Width** from the revealed sub-menu and type in the new column width (11 in this case).

Now edit the copied headings 'Jan', 'Feb', 'Mar', and '1st Qrt' to 'Apr', 'May', 'Jun', and '2nd Qrt'.

Note that by the time the highlighted bar is moved to column I, the 'titles' in column A have scrolled to the left and are outside the viewing screen area. This will make editing of numeric information very difficult if we can't see what refers to what. Therefore, before we attempt any further editing, it would be a good idea to use the 'Title' command ability of SuperCalc to freeze the titles in column A of our present spreadsheet.

Freezing Titles on Screen:
To freeze row (or column) headings on a spreadsheet, move the cell pointer a cell below (or to the right) the row (or column) which you want to freeze the titles on the screen, and type **/Title** and press

H (V or B)   to select **Horizontal**, **Vertical** (or **Both**)

which automatically set the headings above (or to the left) of the cell pointer's current position. Moving around the spreadsheet, leaves the headings frozen on the screen. This command is also effective on different window displays of the screen, as will be discussed later. To clear such frozen titles from your spreadsheet, type **/Title Clear.**

Now implement the above changes and edit the numeric information in your spreadsheet into what is shown overleaf.

Note: If you examine this spreadsheet carefully, you will notice that two errors have occurred; one of these has to do with the average calculation of costs in column J – they are in fact identical to those of the first quarter, while the other has to do with the accumulated values in the second quarter.

	A	F	G	H	I	J	K	
1	PROJECT A							
2								
3		Apr	May	Jun	2nd Qrt	Average		
4		==========	==========	==========	==========	==========		
5	Consult:	£15,500.00	£16,000.00	£16,500.00	£48,000.00	£15,500.00		
6		==========	==========	==========	==========	==========		
7	Costs:							
8	Wages	3500	4000	4500	12000	£3,000.00		
9	Travel	500	550	580	1630	£500.00		
10	Rent	300	300	300	900	£300.00		
11	Heat/Lght	150	120	100	370	£166.67		
12	Phone/Fax	300	350	400	1050	£300.00		
13	Adverts	1250	1300	1350	3900	£1,200.00		
14		----------	----------	----------	----------	----------		
15	Tot Cost:	6000	6620	7230	19850	£5,466.67		
16		==========	==========	==========	==========	==========		
17	Profit:	9500	9380	9270	28150	£10,033.33		
18		==========	==========	==========	==========	==========		
19	Cumulat:	9500	18880	28150				
20		==========	==========	==========	==========	==========		

Non-Contiguous Address Range:
The calculations of average values in column J of the previous
spreadsheet are wrong because the range values in the formula
are still those entered for the first quarter only. To correct these,
highlight cell J5 and edit the formula shown in the 'Entry line'
from AVG(B5:D5) to

```
AVG(B5:D5,F5:H5)
```

which on pressing 'Enter' changes the value shown in cell J5.
Note the way the argument of the function is written when
non-contiguous address ranges are involved. Here we have two
contiguous address ranges B5:D5 and F5:H5 which we separate
with a comma.

   Now replicate the formula to the J8:J13 cell range by
highlighting cell J5 and typing **/Copy**, then pressing

Enter	to accept range to copy from
Down arrow	to select beginning of target area
.	(period) to anchor beginning of target area
Down arrow	to highlight target area
Enter	to confirm selection.

Relative and Absolute Cell Addresses:
Entering a mathematical expression into SuperCalc, such as the formula in cell C19 which was

```
B19+C17
```

causes SuperCalc to interpret it as 'add the contents of cell one column to the left of the current position, to the contents of cell two rows above the current position'. In this way, when the formula was later replicated into cell address D19, the contents of the cell relative to the left position of D19 (i.e. C19) and the contents of the cell two rows above it (i.e. D17) was used, instead of the original cell addresses entered in C19. This is relative addressing.

In the formula we want to include in cell E19, we want SuperCalc to interpret the cell addresses of the two specific cells mentioned in it as absolute. For example, writing

```
E5-E15
```

in cell E19 will be interpreted as relative addresses, but

```
$E$5-$E$15
```

is interpreted as absolute addresses. The $ sign must prefix both the column reference and the row reference. Mixed cell addressing is permitted; as for example when a column address reference is needed to be taken as absolute, while a row address reference is needed to be taken as relative. In such a case, the column letter is prefixed by the $ sign.

Now type into cell E19 both versions of the formula; relative addressing first and then absolute addressing and note the difference. Finally, correct the formula in cell F19 in order to obtain the correct results shown overleaf.

The /Move Command:
To improve the printed output of the above example, move the caption to somewhere in the middle of the spreadsheet so that it is centrally placed when we print it out. To do this, highlight cell A1 and type **/Move,** then press

Enter	to select default range to move
Right arrow	to select target range (say D1..D1)
Enter	to confirm target range and execute.

Now press the 'Home' key and save the resultant spreadsheet as PROJECT4.

	A	B	C	D	E	F	G	H	I	J
1										
2										
3					PROJECT ANALYSIS: ADEPT CONSULTANTS LTD					
4		Jan	Feb	Mar	1st Qrt	Apr	May	Jun	2nd Qrt	Average
5	Consult:	£14,000.00	£15,000.00	£16,000.00	£45,000.00	£15,500.00	£16,000.00	£16,500.00	£48,000.00	£15,500.00
6										
7	Costs:									
8	Wages	2000	3000	4000	9000	3500	4000	4500	12000	£3,500.00
9	Travel	400	500	600	1500	500	550	580	1630	£521.67
10	Rent	300	300	300	900	300	300	300	900	£300.00
11	Heat/Lght	150	-200	150	500	150	120	100	370	£145.00
12	Phone/Fax	250	300	350	900	300	350	400	1050	£325.00
13	Adverts	1100	1200	1300	3600	1250	1300	1350	3900	£1,250.00
14										
15	Tot Cost:	4200	6500	6700	16400	6000	6620	7230	19850	£6,041.67
16										
17	Profit:	9800	9500	9300	28600	9500	9380	9270	28150	£9,458.33
18										
19	Cumulat:	9800	19300	28600	28600	38100	47480	56750		
20										

The /Window Command:
You can use the **/Window** command to save time and effort when working with a large spreadsheet. Just as the **/Title** command, **/Window** segments the screen, but this time into either vertical or horizontal sub-displays. By using **/Window** you can access all of the following options:

Horizontal Vertical Clear Synchronize Unsynchronized

The **Horizontal** and **Vertical** options split the screen at the current column or row location of the highlighted bar. The **Clear** option clears the right or lower window and completes the display from the left or upper screen. The **Synchronize** option allows both windows to move in unison when the highlighted bar is moved. With a vertical split, both screens adjust when the highlighted bar is moved up or down at the edge of the screen, while for a horizontal split, this movement happens when the highlighted bar is moved left or right, again, at the edge of the screen. Using the **Unsynchronized** option allows each screen to be scrolled independently.

To move between screens, press **F6,** or the semicolon (**;**). The position of the highlighted bar of each window screen is stored each time **F6** is used so that moving back to a window, returns you to the last position you were at before changing screens. As a result of this ability, SuperCalc allows you to work on different parts of very large spreadsheets easily and quickly.

As an example of using the **/Window** command, load the PROJECT4 spreadsheet and move the highlighted bar to cell C1, then type **/Window Vertical,** then use

Right Arrow	to bring columns I and J into view
F6	to move the highlighted bar to the left window
Right Arrow	to bring column E into view.

The resultant display should be as shown overleaf. Should you now use the Down Arrow, the highlighted bar will move downwards within the left window, eventually causing the contents of the left screen to scroll upwards, while the contents of the right screen remain unmoved. If you press 'Home' to return the highlighted bar to the A1 cell, and then press **/Window Synchronize,** any subsequent use of the down or up arrows scroll both windows in unison.

To remove the window split of the screen, use the **/Window Clear** command.

	A	E		I	J	K	L	M	
1		LYSIS: ADEP	1						
2			2						
3		1st Qrt	3	2nd Qrt	Average				
4	=======================	4	====================					
5	Consult:	£45,000.00	5	£48,000.00	£15,500.00				
6	=======================	6	====================					
7	Costs:		7						
8	Wages	9000	8	12000	£3,500.00				
9	Travel	1500	9	1630	£521.67				
10	Rent	900	10	900	£300.00				
11	Heat/Lght	500	11	370	£145.00				
12	Phone/Fax	900	12	1050	£325.00				
13	Adverts	3600	13	3900	£1,250.00				
14	-------------------------	14	----------------------					
15	Tot Cost:	16400	15	19850	£6,041.67				
16	=======================	16	====================					
17	Profit:	28600	17	28150	£9,458.33				
18	=======================	18	====================					
19	Cumulat:	28600	19	56750					
20	=======================	20	====================					

Multipage Spreadsheet:

A multipage spreadsheet can be used when you are working with information which is related, and which will be convenient to save together under one filename. In effect, a multipage spreadsheet emulates a three-dimensional spreadsheet so that, in addition to the two dimensions of rows and columns, each spreadsheet can have many pages up to a limit of 255, the upper limit being dependent on available RAM memory in your system.

SuperCalc offers several ways of optimizing memory. For example, using the **/Global Optimum Next** command, provides the possibility of choosing one of the following options:

Memory	which allows selection of **Fast** for fast program execution or **Data-space** for saving memory
Boundary	which allows you to increase data-space by selecting a smaller spreadsheet size
Graphics	which allows selection of **No** for disabling graphics and so freeing some more memory

The **Undo** option will be disabled automatically, should the available memory be not sufficient enough for the size of spreadsheet you are trying to create. If this happens, a message to that effect will appear on the screen.

Each page of a multipage spreadsheet is given a number, so that reference to the cell A11 in page two, say, is now made by 2!A11. Referring to pages in formulae is a simple matter of adding the page prefix, which forms a link between pages. Separate pages of a spreadsheet can be formatted in completely different ways, so that corresponding page columns, for example, can have different widths in different pages. Such a multipage spreadsheet is saved as a single file, although it is possible to have several files open at once and create links between them, whether these files are all in memory or not. The upper limit of open files is still 255, although this is purely academic as your system is likely to have run out of memory long before that.

Moving from one page to another in a multipage spreadsheet is simple enough. Just press **Ctrl-Gray +** to go to the next higher numbered page, and **Ctrl-Gray −** to move back one page (both the plus and minus being the ones on the gray keys of the numeric pad). When a spreadsheet contains several pages, it is possible to view several pages simultaneously to a maximum of three pages. To view parts of such pages on screen you could use the **//Spreadsheets Display** command and then select one of the following options:

1 2 3 Synchronize Unsynchronize Zoom

Choices 1, 2 and 3 control the number of pages to be displayed simultaneously on screen. The **Synchronize** option, which is also the default multi-spreadsheet mode, displays the current spreadsheet page and two adjacent ones. Moving from one page to another causes synchronized movement in spreadsheets displayed in other windows, while **Unsynchronize** has the opposite effect. The **Zoom** option allows you to toggle between multipage and single page display. However, once the number of pages to be displayed simultaneously has been specified, using **Ctrl-F7** is the easiest method of toggling between multipage and single page display.

In order to gain some insight into multipage spreadsheets, we need to create one. The easiest way of doing this is by loading the spreadsheet saved under the filename PROJECT4 and changing it appropriately from a single-page spreadsheet to multipage spreadsheet. By default, all the examples created so far were single-page spreadsheets.

Creating a multipage spreadsheet:

Before you can create a multipage spreadsheet, make sure you have enough RAM memory. If your system has only the standard memory of 640KB, then implement the suggestions discussed in the previous section, on how to release extra memory. Having done this, load the PROJECT4 file and choose the **Replace** option. Then, use the **/Delete** command to first delete column J, followed by columns B to E, then delete rows 19 to 20, and type the new heading in the first row, so that the final display is as shown below:

```
        A        B          C          D          E       F        G
1              DETAILS 2ND QUARTER
2
3                 Apr        May        Jun      2nd Qrt
4           ================================================
5    Consult:   £15,500.00 £16,000.00 £16,500.00 £48,000.00
6           ================================================
7    Costs:
8    Wages       3500       4000       4500      12000
9    Travel      500        550        580       1630
10   Rent        300        300        300        900
11   Heat/Lght   150        120        100        370
12   Phone/Fax   300        350        400       1050
13   Adverts     1250       1300       1350      3900
14           -----------------------------------------------
15   Tot Cost:   6000       6620       7230      19850
16           ================================================
17   Profit:     9500       9380       9270      28150
18           ================================================
19
20
```

Now, press the 'Home' key and use the **/Insert Page** command to insert a page before page 1, which for this example, is the current page. On execution of this last keystroke, a new page 1 is inserted in front of the current page, the latter being automatically renumbered to 2. Again, while in new page 1, load the PROJECT4 file, but this time use the **All** option. Then, delete columns F to J and rows 19 to 20, and type in the new heading in the first row, so that the final displayed screen is as follows:

1	A	B	C	D	E	F	G	
1		DETAILS 1ST QUARTER						
2								
3			Jan	Feb	Mar	1st Qrt		
4		==						
5	Consult:	£14,000.00	£15,000.00	£16,000.00	£45,000.00			
6		==						
7	Costs:							
8	Wages	2000	3000	4000	9000			
9	Travel	400	500	600	1500			
10	Rent	300	300	300	900			
11	Heat/Lght	150	200	150	500			
12	Phone/Fax	250	300	350	900			
13	Adverts	1100	1200	1300	3600			
14		---						
15	Tot Cost:	4200	5500	6700	16400			
16		==						
17	Profit:	9800	9500	9300	28600			
18		==						
19								
20								

Finally, press the 'Home' key and use the **/Insert Page** command once more, to insert one extra page in front of the current page, and reload PROJECT4 into it. Then, delete columns F to H first, followed by columns B to D. The remaining columns on this page will now be displaying the entry ERROR. This is because all three columns rely on information which is on the other two pages. To rectify this, highlight cell B5 and press the **F2** function key to edit its contents. What appears in the entry line now is

SUM(ERROR:ERROR)

which should be edited to

SUM(2!B5:D5)

where the 2! refers to the second page. You will, most certainly, find it necessary to increase the width of columns B through F to 12 characters in order to accommodate the suggested format. This method of entering information, provides a link between different pages of a spreadsheet. Now, copy the edited formula into the cell range B8:B13, and then edit the formula in cell C5, which should be

```
SUM(3!B5:D5)
```

where the 3! refers to the third page. Now copy this formula into the cell range C8:C13, and appropriately edit other cells, as necessary, so that after deleting rows 19 to 20, the display of the contents of page 1, looks as follows:

1	A	B	C	D	E	F	
1		PROJECT ANALYSIS: ADEPT CONSULTANTS LTD					
2							
3		1st Qrt	2nd Qrt	3rd Qrt	4th Qrt	Average	
4	===						
5	Consult:	£45,000.00	£48,000.00			£15,500.00	
6	===						
7	Costs:						
8	Wages	£9,000.00	£1,200.00			£3,500.00	
9	Travel	£1,500.00	£1,630.00			£521.67	
10	Rent	£900.00	£900.00			£300.00	
11	Heat/Lght	£500.00	£370.00			£145.00	
12	Phone/Fax	£900.00	£1,050.00			£325.00	
13	Adverts	£3,600.00	£3,900.00			£1,250.00	
14	--						
15	Tot Cost:	£16,400.00	£19,850.00			£6,041.67	
16	===						
17	Profit:	£28.600.00	£28,150.00			£9,458.33	
18	===						
19							
20							

Before going any further, save this spreadsheet under the filename PROJECT5. To step forward to the next page from the current page, use the **Ctrl-Gray +** keystroke, or to see all three pages at once, use the **//Spreadsheets Display** command and then select **3** from the available options. The display should now change to what is shown on the next page. To toggle between multipage and single page display, or vice versa, use the **Ctrl-F7** keystroke.

As it can be seen, having three pages on display at the same time, tends to cut down the amount you can see from each, but for some applications doing just that can be very helpful. If you want to see more, the current page can be windowed further, either horizontally or vertically, the windows remaining intact as you step from one page into another.

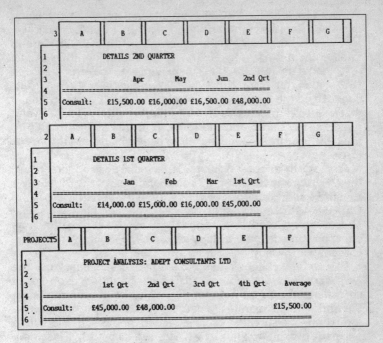

3	A	B	C	D	E	F	G

DETAILS 2ND QUARTER

		Apr	May	Jun	2nd Qrt

Consult: £15,500.00 £16,000.00 £16,500.00 £48,000.00

2	A	B	C	D	E	F	G

DETAILS 1ST QUARTER

		Jan	Feb	Mar	1st Qrt

Consult: £14,000.00 £15,000.00 £16,000.00 £45,000.00

PROJECCT5	A	B	C	D	E	F

PROJECT ANALYSIS: ADEPT CONSULTANTS LTD

	1st Qrt	2nd Qrt	3rd Qrt	4th Qrt	Average

Consult: £45,000.00 £48,000.00 £15,500.00

Pages containing sensitive information can be hidden from
view with the **//Spreadsheets Hide** command, followed by the
page number, if you want to hide one particular page, or the
spreadsheet name if you want to hide all the pages of a
particular spreadsheet. However, you can not hide all the pages
of a particular spreadsheet, if that spreadsheet is the only one
resident in memory.

Multiple Spreadsheets:
We refer to multiple spreadsheets as spreadsheets which use
inter-spreadsheet formulae. Such spreadsheets can either be
resident in memory (open) or they can be on disc. Some or all of
these multiple spreadsheets can have more than one page.
Again, the only limitation on how complicated your application
is, depends primarily on available memory.

To demonstrate the use of multiple spreadsheets, load the
PROJECT5 file and then save each page under the abbreviated
names PROJ5A, PROJ5B and PROJ5C. For example, the first
page can be saved using the **/Save PROJ5A Single 1 All**
command.

Now, first load the PROJ5C spreadsheet into memory, using the **/Load Replace** command, then use the **Ctrl-Enter** keystroke, followed by the **/Load All** command, to load the PROJ5B file, and finally repeat the last two commands to load the PROJ5A file.

Note that the PROJ5A file is displayed with the error message **N/A,** which stands for 'Not Available', indicating that SuperCalc cannot find the file to which reference is made in a formula in that cell. To eliminate this error, highlight cell B5 of PROJ5A and press the **F2** key to edit the formula in that cell from 2!E5 to PROJ5B!E5. Similarly, edit all other cells which contain the **N/A** error message.

To see all three spreadsheets displayed at once on screen, use the **//Spreadsheets Display 3** command. Use of the **Ctrl-Gray +** keystroke allow rotation between spreadsheets, while use of the **Ctrl-F7** keystroke allows the display to change between single and multiple spreadsheets. These two keystrokes have the same effect on spreadsheets, as they had on pages, when a multipage spreadsheet was in use earlier on.

To save any changes made to loaded spreadsheets, use the **//Spreadsheets Save** command. This command saves on disc all spreadsheets currently in memory which have been modified, but under their separate file names. To exit the program, when more than one spreadsheet is loaded in memory, or more than one page of a multipage spreadsheet is displayed on the screen, use the **//Spreadsheets Quit Y** command.

Finally, re-enter SuperCalc and load the PROJ5A file by itself. You will find that the disc drive operates somewhat longer than usual, because a summary information of all spreadsheet links found in the current spreadsheet and those on other files on disc is being prepared. While this process takes place, the message 'Linking ...' appears on the second line of the dialogue panel. This information can be displayed on screen by using the **Ctrl-F3** keystroke; it is known as the Reference Spreadsheet Directory. In this way, links can be established between a spreadsheet resident in memory and other very large spreadsheets which can only be resident on disc, because of memory limitations.

ADDING SPREADSHEET GRAPHS

SuperCalc allows you to represent information in graphical form which makes data more accessible to non-expert users who might not be familiar with the spreadsheet format. In any case, the well known saying 'a picture is worth a thousand words', applies equally well to graphs and figures.

SuperCalc allows over 100 two- and three-dimensional chart and graph types, including bar, stacked bar, pie, area and polar graphs. Charts and Graphs can be grouped, clustered and overlapped. Although there are only nine different main graph-types which can be selected from the Graphics Options menu, namely,

Bar Pie Dual Line Area Hi-Lo X-Y Radar Word

there are many more options that are available within each type (31 in total). In addition, SuperCalc allows the selection of 3-D and horizontal orientation for many of these graphs. Finally, you can add to them titles, legends, labels, and can select grids, fill types, scaling, fonts, etc. These graphs (you can have several per spreadsheet) can be displayed on the screen and can be sent to an appropriate output device, such as a plotter or printer. Although this module rivals a stand alone graphics package, and one could write a separate book on it, an attempt will be made to present its basics, in the space allotted to it.

The nine main graph-types are normally used when we would like to describe the following relationships between data:

Bar	for comparing differences in data — Stacked-Bars are used for comparing cumulative data,
Pie	for comparing parts with the whole,
Dual	for relating two levels of detail about a data element,
Line	for showing changes is data,
Area	for showing a volume relationship between two series,
Hi-Lo	for showing the extreme high and low values for each point in two or more series of values — useful for opening and closing trading figures in shares,
XY	for showing relationships between X and Y,
Radar	for plotting one series of data as angle values defined in radians against one or more series defined in terms of a radius, and
Word	for showing words in the graph environment.

Graphs can not be displayed at the same time as the spreadsheet because graphs use the graphics mode of your computer while worksheets use the text mode. Nevertheless, once the preliminary definition of data is made and selection of the type of graph you would like to see, doing so is quite easy. As graphs are dynamic, any changes made to the data are automatically reflected on the defined graphs.

Preparing for a Line Graph:
In order to illustrate some of the graphing capabilities of SuperCalc, we will now plot the income from consultancies graph of the PROJECT4 file. First we need to define the type of graph to be displayed followed by the range of the data we want to graph. However, the specified range of data to be graphed must be contiguous for each graph. But in our example, the range of data is split into two areas; Jan-Mar (occupying cell positions B3..D3), and Apr-Jun (occupying cell positions F3..H3), with the corresponding income values in cells B5..D5 and F5..H5. Thus, to create an appropriate contiguous data range, we must first replicate the labels and values of these two range areas in another area of the spreadsheet (say, beginning in cell B21 for the actual month labels and B22 for the values of the corresponding income).

Before you start, however, consider what will happen if you used the **/Copy** only command for this replication. If these cells contained formulae, using the **/Copy** only command would cause the relative cell addresses to adjust to the new locations and each formula will then recalculate a new value for each cell which will give wrong results.

The /Copy No-adjust Command:
The **/Copy No-adjust** command copies only cell references without adjusting to new location. To do this, make sure that PROJECT4 is your current spreadsheet and that the mode indicator is on 'READY', move the highlighted bar over the cell forming the beginning of a range to be copied (B3 in this case), and then use the **/Copy** command and press

	(period) to anchor the beginning of the range
Arrows	to highlight entire range (Jan to Mar)
Enter	to confirm range selection, at which point you'll be asked to enter range to copy to
Arrows	to highlight beginning of area to copy data range to (B21 in this case)
,	(comma) to select Copy Options
N	to select **No-adjust** which copies cell references without adjusting to new location
Enter	to confirm and execute the copy of data.

Now repeat the same procedure for labels Apr-Jun, but copy them into E21 to form a contiguous data range. Then do the same with the consultancy values, placing them in adjacent columns in the row below the months (starting in cell B22). Finally, clear the Title protection and add labels for 'Months' and 'Income' in cells A21 and A22, as shown below.

	A	B	C	D	E	F	G	
3		Jan	Feb	Mar	1st Qrt	Apr	May	
4		=====	=====	=====	=====	=====	=====	
5	Consult:	£14,000.00	£15,000.00	£16,000.00	£45,000.00	£15,500.00	£16,000.00	
6		=====	=====	=====	=====	=====	=====	
7	Costs:							
8	Wages	2000	3000	4000	9000	3500	4000	
9	Travel	400	500	600	1500	500	550	
10	Rent	300	300	300	900	300	300	
11	Heat/Lght	150	200	150	500	150	120	
12	Phone/Fax	250	300	350	900	300	350	
13	Adverts	1100	1200	1300	3600	1250	1300	
14		-----	-----	-----	-----	-----	-----	
15	Tot Cost:	4200	5500	6700	16400	6000	6620	
16		=====	=====	=====	=====	=====	=====	
17	Profit:	9800	9500	9300	28600	9500	9380	
18		=====	=====	=====	=====	=====	=====	
19	Cumulat:	9800	19300	28600	28600	38100	47480	
20		=====	=====	=====	=====	=====	=====	
21	Months	Jan	Feb	Mar	Apr	May	Jun	
22	Income	£14,000.00	£15,000.00	£16,000.00	£15,500.00	£16,000.00	£16,500.00	

The //Graphics Command:

We can now proceed with the definition of the type of graph to be drawn. To do this, make sure that the mode indicator is on 'READY' and use the **//Graphics** command. If the message 'Graphics not enabled' appears on your screen, your graphics capability must have been disabled to allow more memory to be used for data, perhaps when you were using multiple pages or spreadsheets earlier on.

To enable Graphics, save your current work under the filename PROJECT6, and then type **/Global Optimum Next Graphics Yes Memory Data-space Quit** then, to keep the changes for future sessions, type **/Global Keep Yes** and quit SuperCalc.

41

Now re-enter SuperCalc, load PROJECT6 and type **//Graphics Type Line** which allows selection of the type of graph or chart to be drawn (Line in this case). SuperCalc, then returns you to the Graphics menu at which you type **Labels Axis-labels** which causes the AXIS LABELS OPTION MENU to appear on the screen.

Move to the X-Axis column and type B21:G21, then press

Enter	to confirm selection
Esc	to return to the **Labels** sub-menu
Q	to **Quit** and return to the Graphics menu.

Now, type **Data** which causes the CHART DATA APPEARANCE AND OPTIONS MENU to be displayed, with 5 series ranges appearing on the screen. There another 5 ranges which can be reached by using the Right Arrow key. In series 1, type B22:G22, press 'Enter' followed by 'Esc'. The cursor at this point is over the Graphics menu option **View,** which means that by pressing the 'Enter' key the defined graph can be viewed.

At this point, your screen should clear and a line graph, as shown below, should appear on it.

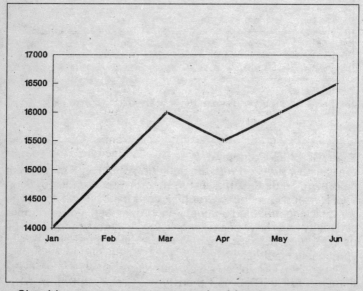

Should your computer respond with an error message instead, then you must have made a mistake when defining either the type of graph or the data ranges. If that happens, then press the 'Esc' key to return to the Graph menu, use **Z** to select **Zap** and start again.

If you don't use **Zap** you will find that SuperCalc remembers the previously defined range settings, which might be rather useful to you if you are defining another graph type which uses the same range settings. Once the correct graph has been successfully displayed on screen, you can 'name' it for future use.

Saving Graphs:
To name a graph, use the **Name** command from within the Graphics menu which will display a sub-menu. This is a list of options which lets you **Retrieve, Store, Delete** or **Zap** a graph name. Select Store which will prompt you for a graph name. In this case, type INCOME and press 'Enter'.

The named setting of the last graph remain the current, and when you select new settings, the current ones are presented as default so that you can reuse as many of these as you like. This reduces the time required to define new settings for a graph that happens to be rather similar to one you have already defined.

Now save the spreadsheet under the filename PROJECT6. This will ensure that your named graphs are also saved under the spreadsheet name. You can save as many separate graphs with the same spreadsheet filename as you like, provided you gave each one a different 'name', using the **//Graphics Name Store** command. As an example, with the settings of the INCOME graph as current, we only need to type **//Graphics Type Bar View** to view the same information in barchart appearance. Use the **Name Store** command to save this new graph under the name INCOME_BAR.

To select any graph and make it the current graph, use the **Name Retrieve** command and press the **F3** function key to see a list of the saved names of charts. Use the arrow keys to highlight the required name from the list, then press 'Enter' to select it as the current chart.

Labels and Titles:
There are several options within the **//Graphics Labels** menu which allow you to add information on your graph, such as Axis-labels, Legend-labels, Data-labels and Titles. The **//Graphics Labels Legend-labels** command, invokes the LEGEND LABEL DEFINITION AND OPTIONS MENU which allows you to specify the wording of a legend which appears on the X-axis of your graph.

In the case of our INCOME...BAR example, this would be 'Income'. Use the **F4** function key to point to cell A22 and press 'Enter'. What appears on your screen is shown below.

```
                    LEGEND LABEL DEFINITION AND OPTIONS MENU        TYPE: BAR

LEGEND LABEL RANGE          A22

LEGEND LOCATION
  Position                  UpperRight
  Placement                 Outside

LEGEND LABEL OPTIONS
  Color                     Black
  Font                      Auto
  Size                      Auto
  Justify                   Auto
  Format                    General
  Date Format               D1


LEGEND BOX
  Display                   Yes
  Color                     White
  Outline                   Black



  33>//Graphics,Labels,Legend-labels,
MENU  F4:Point
```

The positioning of the legend box can be changed from the default 'UpperRight' position and 'Outside' placement to just about anywhere on the chart by simply overriding the default values shown above. You can also change the colour, point size, font, justification, format or date format of the legend labels. Having made your selection, press 'Esc' to return to the Graphics Labels menu.

The **//Graphics Labels Titles** command, invokes the TITLES ENTRY MENU which allows you to add a top title, a subtitle and a footnote to the whole graph, annotate the X, Y1 and Y2 axes, and provide a legend title. Add the suggested titles so that what appears on your screen is as shown on the next page. A second screen allows you to specify colour, font, size, justification and positioning of titles, axis annotation and legend title. This screen is reached from the previous screen by pressing 'PgDn'

```
                     TITLES ENTRY MENU                    TYPE: BAR    ↓

TOP TITLE 1    ADEPT CONSULTANTS
          2    Monthly Income
          3

SUBTITLE  1
          2

FOOTNOTE  1
          2
          3

AXIS TITLES
     X-Axis    Months in 1989
     Y1-Axis   Consultancy Income
     Y2-Axis

LEGEND TITLE   Consultancy



   26>//Graphics,Labels,Titles,
 MENU  F4:Point  F5:Row/Col  PgDn:Options
```

Having made your selections, press 'Esc' to return to the
Graphics Labels menu. Again, the cursor at this point is over the
Graphics menu option **View** and therefore, pressing 'Enter',
clears the screen and displays the latest defined barchart.

Drawing a Multiple Barchart:
As an additional exercise, define graph settings for a new
bar-type graph which deals with the monthly 'Costs' of Adept
Consultants. As there are six different non-contiguous sets of
costs, you must first copy them (including the cost description
labels) into a contiguous range below the 'Income' range
(starting, say, at cell A24), then use the **//Graphics Data** command
to invoke the CHART DATA APPEARANCE AND OPTIONS
MENU into which you must specify, for the first six series
ranges, the corresponding costs. Use the **F4** function key to
point to the cost range category within the spreadsheet. When
this is completed, use the **Labels Legend-labels** option of the
Graphics menu to invoke the LEGEND DEFINITION AND
OPTIONS MENU and use the **F4** function key to select the
appropriate range, say, A24:A29.

45

In this way, 6 different bars (corresponding to the six different costs) can be plotted for each month, appropriately annotated so that the different crosshatching patterns which represent the different cost categories can be distinguished clearly. Now, give a title to your graph and use the **Name Store** command to save the barchart under the filename COSTS before viewing it. The completed graph should look as follows:

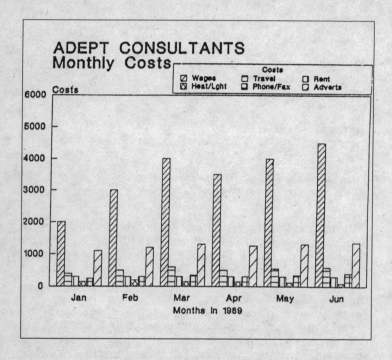

You can view the same chart in three dimension by simply selecting **Options** from the Graphics menu which invokes the BAR CHART OPTIONS MENU and change the entry under 3D from 'No' to 'Yes'. Then, use the **Name Store** command to save the barchart under the filename COSTS...3D before viewing it. The completed graph should look as shown on the next page.

Finally, save the graphs in the current worksheet by saving the spreadsheet under the filename PROJECT6.

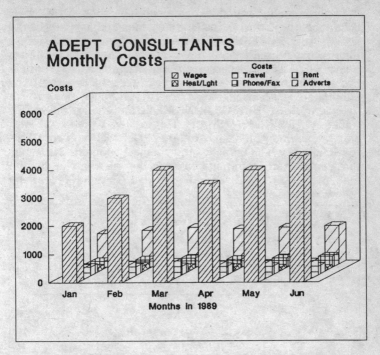

ADEPT CONSULTANTS
Monthly Costs

Costs
☑ Wages   ☐ Travel   ☐ Rent
☒ Heat/Lght   ☐ Phone/Fax   ☐ Adverts

Costs

Months in 1989

Drawing a Pie Chart:
As a second example, use the 'Average' values of the costs from the spreadsheet of PROJECT6 to plot a pie chart. Again define the new graph type as 'Pie' and then choose the **Data** option from the Graphics menu to invoke the CHART DATA APPEARANCE AND OPTIONS MENU.

Since the barchart representation of the various costs was the last defined series ranges, they are presented as the default values. However, a pie chart needs only the Series 1 range to be defined (in this case J8:J13) and, therefore, all other default values must be removed from the menu. This is best done by highlighting the next five unwanted series ranges and pressing the 'Del' key. If you want to explode a segment of the pie chart, you can do so by changing the 'Pie Explosion' entry in the menu from 'No' to 'Yes'.

In addition. do remember to switch off the 3D option which is active as a result of using the default values of the previously current chart. To do this, choose **Options** from the Graphics menu and change the entry under 3D from 'Yes' to 'No'.

To annotate the segments of the pie chart, choose the **Labels Data-labels** option from the Graphics menu which invokes the DATA LABELS OPTIONS MENU and specify the range of labels (in this case A8:A13). Note, however, that when the pie chart is displayed on screen, a certain amount of clutter exists amongst the annotation of the smallest segments of the chart. To eliminate this, choose **Options** from the Graphics menu which invokes the PIE CHART OPTIONS MENU and change the entries under SORT SEGMENTS from 'No' to 'Yes' which sorts with smallest segments first, and under EXPLOSION Type from 'List' to 'Smallest' which detaches the smallest segment. Now, use the **Name Store** command to save the pie chart under the filename COSTS...PIE and then select **View** to reveal the following display:

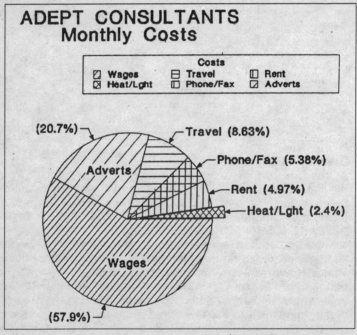

Note that we did not have to use the **Titles** option of the Graphics menu to specify titles for the pie chart, as the last current chart itself had to do with costs and, therefore, the previously defined titles were the default. Finally, save the spreadsheet under the filename PROJECT7, which will also save with it all the charts specified up to now.

48

Creating a Dual Chart:

The dual-charting option is a very powerful technique used for relating two levels of detail. SuperCalc allows you to use dual charts in the following combination: Pie-Bar, Pie-Pie, Bar-Pie and Bar-Bar. Using these combinations you can see how a data element fits within a larger set of data.

As an example of this dual graph technique, we will choose as the left graph a pie chart to show the three segments of our imaginary company; income, costs and profit, and the right graph as a bar chart to show the details of the costs segment. To do this, we will use the PROJECT7 spreadsheet and use the **/Copy No-adjust** command to copy the 'Average' six-monthly values for 'Income', 'Costs' and 'Profit' from columns J5, J15 and J17, respectively, into range J21:J23. Use the range I21:I23 for the appropriate labels describing the values. Similarly, copy the individual values for 'Costs' from J8:J13 into J24:J29, and their corresponding labels from A24:A29 into I24:I29. That part of the spreadsheet should look as follows:

		Column	
		I	J
	21	Income	£15,500.00
	22	Costs	£6,041.67
	23	Profit	£9,458.33
	24	Wages	£3,500.00
Row	25	Travel	£521.67
	26	Rent	£300.00
	27	Heat/Lght	£145.00
	28	Phone/Fax	£325.00
	29	Adverts	£1,250.00

Now, activate the graphics module with the **//Graphics** command and use the **Zap** option first, to remove from memory the current chart and, by implication, its default settings. Then, select the **Type** option from the Graphics menu, and choose **Dual,** followed by the **Data** option, and press **F4** to point and highlight J21:J23 for the 1st series range and J24:J29 for the 2nd series range. Also, change the entry under 'Pie Explosion' of the 1st series, from 'No' to 'Yes'.

To define legend labels and titles, first choose the **Labels** option from the Graphics menu, and select **Legend-labels,** and type the range I21:I29. Then select **Titles** and type in the 1st line of TOP TITLE 'Monthly Averages', and in the 2nd line 'Over six-month period'. Finally, select **Options** and change the entries under LINK CHARTS from 'No' to 'Yes' and under EXPLOSION Type from 'List' to 'Smallest'.

Now, use the **Name Store** command to save the dual-chart
under the filename COSTS...DUAL and then select **View** to
reveal the following display:

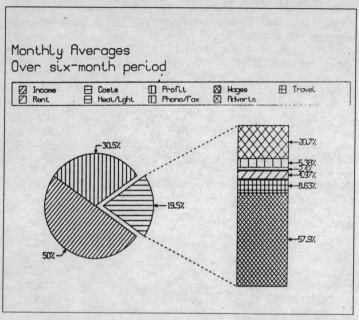

Finally, save the spreadsheet under the filename PROJECT7.

Plotting Graphs:
To plot any of these graphs, simply use the **//Graphics Name
Retrieve** command to make the required chart the current one,
then simply select **Plot** from the Graphics menu. If you have
implemented a plotter, then the output will be sent to the plotter,
otherwise it will be sent to the printer. As most printers can
double as graphics devices, the output you will get from such a
printer can be of very high quality.

You can change the default settings of your various output
devices by using the **//Graphics Global Options** command which
invokes the GLOBAL OPTIONS MENU which allows you to
change options for the Monitor, Printer, Plotter and ViewGraph.
To find out the available options for, say, your printer, highlight
the entry against 'Resolution' and press F1. Since SuperCalc
provides context sensitive help, this is by far the best way of
finding out what is available.

DATABASE MANAGEMENT

A SuperCalc database is a spreadsheet which contains related information, such as 'Customer's Names', 'Consultancy Details', 'Invoice No.' etc. Each database record is entered as a spreadsheet row, with the fields of each record occupying corresponding columns.

Setting-up a Database:

In order to investigate the various database functions, such as sorting, searching, date calculations etc, we first need to setup a spreadsheet in the form shown below.

	A	B	C	D	E	F	G
1		INVOICE ANALYSIS: ADEPT CONSULTANTS LTD				AT 18.08.89	
2							
3	CUSTOMER'S	CONSULTANCY	INV.	DATE OF	P/D	DAYS	TOTAL
4	NAME	DETAILS	No	ISSUE	Y/N	OVER	VALUE
5	===
6	VORTEX Co. Ltd	Wind Tunnel Tests	8901	4.5.89	N		£120.84
7	AVON Construction	Adhesive Tests	8902	11.5.89	Y		£103.52
8	BARROWS Associates	Tunnel Design Tests	8903	13.5.89	N		£99.32
9	STONEAGE Ltd	Carbon Dating Tests	8904	15.5.89	N		£55.98
10	PARKWAY Gravel	Material Size Tests	8905	20.5.89	N		£180.22
11	WESTWOOD Ltd	Load Bearing Tests	8906	20.5.89	N		£68.52
12	GLOWORM Ltd	Luminescence Tests	8907	20.5.89	N		£111.55
13	SILVERSMITH Co	X-Ray Diffract. Test	8908	26.5.89	Y		£123.45
14	WORMGLAZE Ltd	Heat Transfer Tests	8909	29.5.89	N		£35.87
15	EALING Engines Dgn	Vibration Tests	8910	2.6.89	N		£58.95
16	HIRE Service Equip	Network Implement/n	8911	10.6.89	N		£290.00
17	EUROBASE Co. Ltd	Proj. Contr. Manag.	8912	18.6.89	N		£150.00
18	FREEMARKET Dealers	Stock Control Pack.	8913	25.6.89	N		£560.00
19	OILRIG Construct.	Metal Fatigue Tests	8914	3.7.89	N		£96.63
20	TIME & Motion Ltd	Systems Analysis	8915	13.7.89	N		£120.35

We assume that the 'Invoice Analysis' of Adept Consultants is designed and set out as shown above with the field titles and field widths shown on the next page. Use the **/Format Column Width** command to change the width of the various columns to those given, and then enter the abbreviated titles, but use the **/Format Row Text Center Accept** command to position them centrally, in two rows, as shown in the spreadsheet above. These widths were chosen so that the whole of the worksheet could be seen on the screen at once.

Column	Title	Width	Type
A	CUSTOMER'S NAME	19	Default
B	CONSULTANCY DETAILS	20	Default
C	INVOICE No	6	Integer
D	DATE OF ISSUE	9	Date, type 8
E	PAID (Y/N)	3	Default
F	DAYS OVERDUE	6	Integer
G	TOTAL VALUE	9	Currency

Use the **/Format Columns Integer Accept** command to format columns C and F to integral values, then the **/Format Column** command to format column D to date using the **User-defined Date 8** option, and finally, the **/Format Column $** command to format column G to currency, before entering the information in the spreadsheet. Column F will be calculated later using a formula which relies on information in columns D and E. However, for the time being, leave this column empty and, when you complete the other entries, save the result under the filename INVOICE1.

Sorting a Database:
The records within the above database are in the order in which they were entered, with the 'Invoice No' shown in ascending order. However, once records have been entered, we might find it easier to browse through the database if it was sorted in alphabetical order of 'Customer's Name'. SuperCalc has an easy to use sort function which can be accessed as follows:

Place the highlighted bar at the beginning of the sort range (in this case A6), then use the **/Arrange Block** command, and press

.	(period) to anchor beginning of sort range
Arrows	to highlight block to be sorted (A6:I20)
G	to select **Go** and execute the command

which produces the display shown on the next page.

If you now decide to have both a primary and a secondary sort field keys (say you want invoices for the same company to appear in ascending order of invoice number), you don't even have to confirm the sort block range, as SuperCalc remembers these. If you want to reset anyone of these 'remembered' ranges, then choose the appropriate sort function and press 'Esc' to allow redefinition of the specific choice. For the example sited above, use the **/Arrange Block 1stkey** command and enter the range A6:A20, then choose the **Ascending 2nd key** option and enter the range C6:C20. Finally, choose the **Ascending Go** option.

	A	B	C	D	E	F	G	
1		INVOICE ANALYSIS: ADEPT CONSULTANTS LTD			AT 18.08.89			
2								
3	CUSTOMER'S	CONSULTANCY	INV.	DATE OF	P/D	DAYS	TOTAL	
4	NAME	DETAILS	No	ISSUE	Y/N	OVER	VALUE	
5	===							
6	AVON Construction	Adhesive Tests	8902	11.5.89	Y		£103.52	
7	BARROWS Associates	Tunnel Design Tests	8903	13.5.89	N		£99.32	
8	EALING Engines Dgn	Vibration Tests	8910	2.6.89	N		£58.95	
9	EUROBASE Co. Ltd	Proj. Contr. Manag.	8912	18.6.89	N		£150.00	
10	FREEMARKET Dealers	Stock Control Pack.	8913	25.6.89	N		£560.00	
11	GLOWORM Ltd	Luminescence Tests	8907	20.5.89	N		£111.55	
12	HIRE Service Equip	Network Implement/n	8911	10.6.89	N		£290.00	
13	OILRIG Construct.	Metal Fatigue Tests	8914	3.7.89	N		£96.63	
14	PARKWAY Gravel	Material Size Tests	8905	20.5.89	N		£180.22	
15	SILVERSMITH Co	X-Ray Diffract. Test	8908	26.5.89	Y		£123.45	
16	STONEAGE Ltd	Carbon Dating Tests	8904	15.5.89	N		£55.98	
17	TIME & Motion Ltd	Systems Analysis	8915	13.7.89	N		£120.35	
18	VORTEX Co. Ltd	Wind Tunnel Tests	8901	4.5.89	N		£120.84	
19	WESTWOOD Ltd	Load Bearing Tests	8906	20.5.89	N		£68.52	
20	WORMGLAZE Ltd	Heat Transfer Tests	8909	29.5.89	N		£35.87	

Now resort the database in ascending order of 'Invoice No' so that you obtain a display corresponding to the original data entry screen.

Date Arithmetic:
There are several date functions which can be used in SuperCalc to carry out date calculations. For example, typing the function EDAT(18,8,89), returns the European date format of the specific date, while typing NOW (as in cell G1 of the spreadsheet, which has to be formatted to a Date using the **/Format Entry User-defined 8 Accept** command), returns the current date as given by the internal clock.

Another function, the DATEVALUE, allows a date entered in the declared format of the spreadsheet (such as 18.8.89) to be used for calculations. Thus, typing

```
NOW-DATEVALUE("4.5.89") or NOW-DATEVALUE(D6)
```

gives the difference in days (in integral number, if the appropriate cell is formatted for integer numbers) between now and the mentioned date.

We will use these two functions to work out the number of overdue days of the unpaid invoices in our example, by typing in cell F6 the following formula:

```
NOW-DATEVALUE(D6)
```

If the record in row 6 of the spreadsheet refers to the data of VORTEX Co. Ltd., then the result should be 106 days. However, before we proceed to copy the above formula to the rest of the F column of the database data block, we should take into consideration the fact that, normally, such information is not necessary if an invoice has been paid. Therefore, we need to edit the above formula in such a way as to make the result conditional to non-payment of the issued invoice.

The IF Function:
The IF function allows comparison between two values with the use of a special 'logical' operators. The logical operators we can use are listed below.

Logical operators
=	Equal to
<	Less than
>	Greater than
<=	Less than or Equal to
>=	Greater than or Equal to
<>	Not Equal to

The general format of the IF function is as follows:

IF(Comparison,Outcome-if-true,Outcome-if-false)

which contains three arguments separated by commas. The first argument is the logical comparison, the second is what should happen if the outcome of the logical comparison is 'true', while the third is what should happen if the outcome of the logical comparison is false.

Thus, we can incorporate the IF function in the formula we entered in cell F6 to calculate the days overdue only if the invoice has not been paid, otherwise the string 'N/A' should be written into the appropriate cell should the contents of the corresponding E column of a record be anything else but N. To edit the formula in cell F6, highlight the cell and press the **F2** function key. Then press the 'Home' cursor key to place the cursor at the beginning of the existing formula n the control area at the top of the spreadsheet and insert

```
IF(E6="N",
```

then press the 'End' cursor key to move the cursor to the end of the existing entry and add

```
,"   N/A")
```

The edited formula in cell F6 should now correspond to what is shown below.

```
IF(E6="N",NOW-DATEVALUE(D6),"   N/A")
```

Now copy this formula to the rest of the appropriate range (F7..F20) and compare your results with those shown below.

	A	B	C	D	E	F	G
1		INVOICE ANALYSIS: ADEPT CONSULTANTS LTD				AT	18.08.89
2							
3	CUSTOMER'S	CONSULTANCY	INV.	DATE OF	P/D	DAYS	TOTAL
4	NAME	DETAILS	No	ISSUE	Y/N	OVER	VALUE
5	==						
6	VORTEX Co. Ltd	Wind Tunnel Tests	8901	4.5.89	N	106	£120.84
7	AVON Construction	Adhesive Tests	8902	11.5.89	Y	N/A	£103.52
8	BARROWS Associates	Tunnel Design Tests	8903	13.5.89	N	97	£99.32
9	STONEAGE Ltd	Carbon Dating Tests	8904	15.5.89	N	95	£55.98
10	PARKWAY Gravel	Material Size Tests	8905	20.5.89	N	90	£180.22
11	WESTWOOD Ltd	Load Bearing Tests	8906	20.5.89	N	90	£68.52
12	GLOWORM Ltd	Luminescence Tests	8907	20.5.89	N	90	£111.55
13	SILVERSMITH Co	X-Ray Diffract. Test	8908	26.5.89	Y	N/A	£123.45
14	WORMGLAZE Ltd	Heat Transfer Tests	8909	29.5.89	N	81	£35.87
15	EALING Engines Dgn	Vibration Tests	8910	2.6.89	N	77	£58.95
16	HIRE Service Equip	Network Implement/n	8911	10.6.89	N	69	£290.00
17	EUROBASE Co. Ltd	Proj. Contr. Manag.	8912	18.6.89	N	61	£150.00
18	FREEMARKET Dealers	Stock Control Pack.	8913	25.6.89	N	54	£560.00
19	OILRIG Construct.	Metal Fatigue Tests	8914	3.7.89	N	46	£96.63
20	TIME & Motion Ltd	Systems Analysis	8915	13.7.89	N	36	£120.35

Your results might differ substantially from the ones shown above, as the NOW function returns different numerical values when used at different dates. To get the same results as those shown, edit the formula in column F and replace the NOW function with DATEVALUE(G1) where G1 causes an 'absolute' reference to be made to the contents of cell G1. Now copy this edited formula to the rest of the F column range and change the contents of cell G1 to "18.8.89.

WARNING: It is important that you enter the date, in cells which will be used later for calculations, in the format that you have specified as your replacement to the default 'Date' format of your spreadsheet. It should be obvious that unless the NOW function, which uses the specified internal format for date, is of the same type as the entered dates in other cells, to which you intend to apply 'date' arithmetic, then the result of such calculations will be incorrect. If you have to change the default 'date' format, then use the **/Format User-defined Date** command and choose the type preferred (we have used **8 Accept**). However, make quite sure that you use the **/Global Keep** command to make such choice permanent. If you don't use the **/Global Keep** command, even if everything appears as it should be this time, when you reload your spreadsheet later, the fields containing the results of 'date' calculations might be in error, because the spreadsheet would have reverted back to its default 'date' format.

After making the above suggested changes to the spreadsheet, save the result under the filename INVOICE2.

Frequency Distribution:

A frequency distribution of data allows us to find how many values in a specified range fall within specified numeric intervals (otherwise known as the bin range).

Thus, if we want to find out how many unpaid invoices exist in our database within 0-30, 31-40, 41-50, etc, days, then we need to specify the bin range in a column of the database and allocate another column to receive the frequency values. We choose to insert two columns between the existing F and G columns of the database by highlighting column G and using the **/Insert Column** command twice. Then, format the two new columns to the widths and numeric types given below:

Column	Title	Width	Type
G	BIN RANGE	5	Integer
H	FREQ DISTRIBUTION	4	Integer

Finally, give the columns the abbreviated headings in two rows, as shown on the next page.

Now enter the values you want to use as intervals for the calculation of the frequency distribution into the bin range column, in this case G6..G20, as shown in the spreadsheet output display on the next page.

To calculate the frequency distribution, highlight cell H6 and use the **//Data Analysis Distribution** command and press

Arrows	to highlight beginning of the data range (F6)
.	(period) to anchor beginning of range
Down arrow	to highlight range (F6..F20)
Enter	to confirm highlighted area
Arrows	to highlight beginning of the bin range (G6)
.	(period) to anchor beginning of range
Down arrow	to highlight range (G6..G20)
Enter	to confirm highlighted area

The result of the frequency distribution is shown below.

	A	B	C	D	E	F	G	H	I
1		INVOICE ANALYSIS: ADEPT CONSULTANTS LTD AT							18.08.89
2									
3	CUSTOMER'S	CONSULTANCY	INV.	DATE OF	P/D	DAYS	BIN	FREQ	TOTAL
4	NAME	DETAILS	No	ISSUE	Y/N	OVER	RAN	DIST	VALUE
5									
6	VORTEX Co. Ltd	Wind Tunnel Tests	8901	4.5.89	N	106	30	0	£120.84
7	AVON Construction	Adhesive Tests	8902	11.5.89	Y	N/A	40	1	£103.52
8	BARROWS Associates	Tunnel Design Tests	8903	13.5.89	N	97	50	1	£99.32
9	STONEAGE Ltd	Carbon Dating Tests	8904	15.5.89	N	95	60	2	£55.98
10	PARKWAY Gravel	Material Size Tests	8905	20.5.89	N	90	70	1	£180.22
11	WESTWOOD Ltd	Load Bearing Tests	8906	20.5.89	N	90	80	2	£68.52
12	GLOWORM Ltd	Luminescence Tests	8907	20.5.89	N	90	90	3	£111.55
13	SILVERSMITH Co	X-Ray Diffract. Test	8908	26.5.89	Y	N/A	100	2	£123.45
14	WORMGLAZE Ltd	Heat Transfer Tests	8909	29.5.89	N	81	110	1	£35.87
15	EALING Engines Dgn	Vibration Tests	8910	2.6.89	N	77	120	0	£58.95
16	HIRE Service Equip	Network Implement/n	8911	10.6.89	N	69	130	0	£290.00
17	EUROBASE Co. Ltd	Proj. Contr. Manag.	8912	18.6.89	N	61	140	0	£150.00
18	FREEMARKET Dealers	Stock Control Pack.	8913	25.6.89	N	54	150	0	£560.00
19	OILRIG Construct.	Metal Fatigue Tests	8914	3.7.89	N	46	160	0	£96.63
20	TIME & Motion Ltd	Systems Analysis	8915	13.7.89	N	36	170	0	£120.35

From the frequency distribution display it can be seen that there are 0 invoices within the period 0-30 days, 1 invoice between the period 31-40 days, 1 between 41-50, 2 between 51-60, etc. Save this spreadsheet under the filename INVOICE3.

Requirement for Searching a Database:
A database can be searched for specific records that meet the criteria established by the use of the //Data Find or //Data Extract command. We will use the database of spreadsheet INVOICE3 to illustrate the method by searching the database with the criterion relating to the frequency distribution of invoices.

Assuming that the database is on your screen, we need to modify it in such a way as to end up with single-row field names and with all subsequent rows containing only records. To achieve this, we need to remove rows 3 and 5 of the database. First highlight row 3, then use the **/Delete Row** command which will eliminate row 3 and shift the rest of the information in the database one row up. Now, highlight the border, which now should be in row 4, and delete it, then edit the field names of columns C and D to INV. and ISSUED, respectively, as shown below.

	A	B	C	D	E	F	G	H	I
1		INVOICE ANALYSIS: ADEPT CONSULTANTS LTD		AT					18.08.89
2									
3	NAME	DETAILS	INV.	ISSUED	Y/N	OVER	RAN	DIST	VALUE
4	VORTEX Co. Ltd	Wind Tunnel Tests	8901	4.5.89	N	106	30	0	£120.84
5	AVON Construction	Adhesive Tests	8902	11.5.89	Y	N/A	40	1	£103.52
6	BARROWS Associates	Tunnel Design Tests	8903	13.5.89	N	97	50	1	£99.32
7	STONEAGE Ltd	Carbon Dating Tests	8904	15.5.89	N	95	60	2	£55.98
8	PARKWAY Gravel	Material Size Tests	8905	20.5.89	N	90	70	1	£180.22
9	WESTWOOD Ltd	Load Bearing Tests	8906	20.5.89	N	90	80	2	£68.52
10	GLOWORM Ltd	Luminescence Tests	8907	20.5.89	N	90	90	3	£111.55
11	SILVERSMITH Co	X-Ray Diffract. Test	8908	26.5.89	Y	N/A	100	2	£123.45
12	WORMGLAZE Ltd	Heat Transfer Tests	8909	29.5.89	N	81	110	1	£35.87
13	EALING Engines Dgn	Vibration Tests	8910	2.6.89	N	77	120	0	£58.95
14	HIRE Service Equip	Network Implement/n	8911	10.6.89	N	69	130	0	£290.00
15	EUROBASE Co. Ltd	Proj. Contr. Manag.	8912	18.6.89	N	61	140	0	£150.00
16	FREEMARKET Dealers	Stock Control Pack.	8913	25.6.89	N	54	150	0	£560.00
17	OILRIG Construct.	Metal Fatigue Tests	8914	3.7.89	N	46	160	0	£96.63
18	TIME & Motion Ltd	Systems Analysis	8915	13.7.89	N	36	170	0	£120.35

There is one more requirement before we can find and/or extract information from a database. This is the setting up of two ranges in the spreadsheet, one for specifying the criteria for the search, and the other for copying records extracted from the database. The latter is only needed if you use the **//Data Extract** command.

To do this, first copy the field names of the database (A3:I3) to an empty area of the spreadsheet, say, A22:I22 which will form the first line of the 'criteria range'. Label this area CRITERIA FOR SEARCHING in cell C1, then setup the second area – the 'output range' – by again copying the field names to A30:I30 and labeling it as OUTPUT RANGE in cell C29, as shown on the next page.

Note that we chose to put the criteria and output ranges in rows below the database rather than on either side of it. This was done so as to avoid the errors that might ensue should we later decide to insert a row in our database, which will also insert a row in the criteria/output range. For a structured spreadsheet layout, see end of chapter.

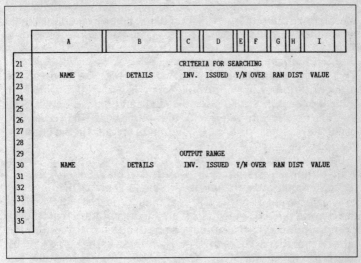

We are now almost ready to search the database. However, before being able to do so, we need to type in the row below the criteria field names (in our example, row 3) the criteria for the search. Assuming that we would like to search the database for all the details of our customers whose invoices fall within a Bin Range of 80 or more days, but whose frequency distribution is greater than 0, then we type in cell G23 the criterion G4>=80 and in cell H23 the criterion H4>0, where G4 and H4 are the appropriate fields of the first record of the database data.

The //Data Find Command:
Before we can use the **//Data Find** command we must specify the input range of our data, which must include the field names (in our example A3:I18), via the **//Data Input** command.

Finally, we need to specify the criterion range, which must include the field names and at least one following row in which the criteria for the search appear (A22:I23 in our case), via the **//Data Criterion** command. Criteria may be included that refer to one field or to several fields.

Do not specify an empty line as part of the criterion range, as this has the effect of searching the database for *all* records. The criteria must be entered in the second and subsequent rows of the criterion range, with each entered below the copy of the appropriate field name. A label or a value may be entered exactly as it appears in the database or the two special characters ? and * can be used to match any single character of a label or all characters to the end of the label. Preceding a label with a tilde (˜), causes the search of all labels except for that one. Thus, ˜Y* searches the database for all records with an entry in that field which does not begin with Y.

To search a database for values, either enter the value as the exact criterion or use a formula, such as G4>=80 in which the logical operators (<, <=, >, >=, <>) can be used. The logical formula generates a value of 1 if the condition is TRUE or a value of 0 if the condition is FALSE. This value appears in the criterion range.

Several criteria can be entered, either in the same row, if you want SuperCalc to search for records that match every criterion (i.e. criteria entered are linked with the logical AND), or one per row, if you want SuperCalc to search records that satisfy any of the criteria (i.e. criteria entered are linked with the logical OR). Compounded logical formulas can be used to create compound criteria that match more than one condition in the same field by using the functions AND(), OR() or NOT() in the formula. For example, had we typed the criterion in G23 as

```
AND(G4>=80,G4<120)
```

and blanked that in H23 (unwanted criteria must be blanked rather than over-typed with a space), we would retrieve the same records that will be retrieved by the use of the two separate criteria, discussed previously.

To search the database for the criteria discussed above, use the **//Data Find** command which causes SuperCalc to highlight the first record that matches the criteria, which in this case is that of WESTWOOD Ltd. Pressing the Down Arrow key finds the next record that matches the chosen criteria. If there are no more records (there should be 4 in all), the message 'No more matching records' is displayed on the screen. You can peruse through the chosen records backwards by pressing the Up Arrow key. Again, if there are no more records that match the chosen criteria, the program displays the 'No more matching records' message when the Up Arrow key is pressed.

The //Data Extract Command:

The **//Data Extract** command copies records that match the chosen criteria from the database to the output range of the spreadsheet. However, before selecting **//Data Extract**, you must use the **//Data Output** command to specify the output range into which data is to be copied. Make sure that the specified output range is sufficiently long to contain all the extracted records. If it is not, the error message 'Output range full; enlarge range and retry' will appear on the screen. In our example, we could specify the output range as A30:I35.

The criteria we used previously with the **//Data Find** command were such that 4 records were found, one of which referred to a customer who had already paid the relevant invoice. To eliminate this customer, add into the criteria selection the entry ˜Y in cell E23 and use the **//Data Extract** command to extract the following records.

	A	B	C	D	E	F	G	H	I
21			CRITERIA FOR SEARCHING						
22	NAME	DETAILS	INV.	ISSUED	Y/N	OVER	RAN	DIST	VALUE
23					˜Y		0	0	
24									
25									
26									
27									
28									
29			OUTPUT RANGE						
30	NAME	DETAILS	INV.	ISSUED	Y/N	OVER	RAN	DIST	VALUE
31	WESTWOOD Ltd	Load Bearing Tests	8906	20.5.89	N	90	80	2	£68.52
32	GLOWORM Ltd	Luminescence Tests	8907	20.5.89	N	90	90	3	£111.55
33	WORMGLAZE Ltd	Heat Transfer Tests	8909	29.5.89	N	81	110	1	£35.87
34									
35									

When the **//Data Extract** command is being executed, the message 'Calculating...' appears is the second line of the dialogue panel of the screen. After the selected records are copied into the output range, selecting **Quit** causes the MENU mode to be exited and you are returned to the READY mode.

Finally, save this spreadsheet under the filename INVOICE4.

Structuring a Spreadsheet:
In a well designed spreadsheet, areas of calculations using formulae which we call reports, must be kept on an entirely separate part of the spreadsheet from the data entry area. The reason for this is to prevent accidental overwriting of formulae that might be contained within a data entry area. If this is adhered to, then the whole spreadsheet can be protected by using the **/Global Protection** command, which switches global protection on for the current spreadsheet, but then the data entry area can be unprotected using the **/Unprotect** command to allow data entry or data change.

Always provide a screen with technical information about the contents of the particular spreadsheet; a kind of an overview of the function of the spreadsheet application. This area must also contain instructions for the use of the particular application at hand. Such information can help others to learn and use an application easily and effectively. If you use range names (these will be discussed in the next chapter), as you *must,* then include a range name table in your information screen(s).

Provide a separate area within a spreadsheet for macros (the subject of the next chapter), which is a Command Language that allows you to chain together menu commands. Use the 'three-column' convention of writing macros (see next chapter). In this way, auditing of this area of your work becomes that much simpler.

To implement the suggested structure, use SuperCalc's multipage ability, as shown in the diagram on the right. However, if your system does not have sufficient memory, then use the structure shown in the diagram below.

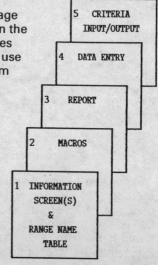

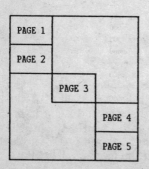

USING MACROS

A macro is a set of instructions made up of a sequence of keystrokes and commands that you would normally have typed onto the keyboard, but which you type instead into your spreadsheet as cell entries. After entering and naming a macro it can be invoked by simply typing its name. Thus, a macro is a list of commands which is used to perform a complete task and is used whenever we wish to save time in performing repetitive commands or make a spreadsheet easier to use.

Creating a Simple Macro:
We will now use the spreadsheet saved under PROJECT3 (see the beginning of the "Adding Spreadsheet Skills chapter) to show how we can add macros to it, to perform 'what-if' type of projections by, say, increasing the 'Wages' bill by 15%. If you haven't saved PROJECT3 on disc, it will be necessary for you to enter the information shown below into SuperCalc so that you can benefit from what is to be introduced at this point. Having done this, do save it under PROJECT3 before going on.

If you have saved PROJECT3, then enter SuperCalc and load the file. What should appear on screen is shown below.

	A	B	C	D	E	F	G
1	PROJECT ANALYSIS: ADEPT CONSULTANTS LTD						
2							
3		Jan	Feb	Mar	1st Qrt	Average	
4	===						
5	Consult:	£14,000.00	£15,000.00	£16,000.00	£45,000.00	£15,000.00	
6	===						
7	Costs:						
8	Wages	2000	3000	4000	9000	£3,000.00	
9	Travel	400	500	600	1500	£500.00	
10	Rent	300	300	300	900	£300.00	
11	Heat/Lght	150	200	150	500	£166.67	
12	Phone/Fax	250	300	350	900	£300.00	
13	Adverts	1100	1200	1300	3600	£1,200.00	
14	---						
15	Tot Cost:	4200	5500	6700	16400	£5,466.67	
16	===						
17	Profit:	9800	9500	9300	28600	£9,533.33	
18	===						
19	Cumulat:	9800	19300	28600			
20	===						

What we would like to do now is to 'Edit' the entries under 'Wages' so that this part of the costs can be increased by 15%. One way of doing this would be to multiply the contents of each cell containing the 'wages' value by 1.15. To do this, we would start by 'editing' the contents of cell B8 by pressing **F2** to 'Edit' the value in it by adding to the entry '*1.15' which has the effect of multiplying the contents of the cell by 1.15 which would increase its contents by 15%. We would then press 'Enter', press the Right Arrow key to move to C8 and repeat the whole procedure. The exact steps, after highlighting cell B8, are:

Manual Procedure	*Equivalent Macro Steps*
Press **F2** to 'Edit' cell	{EDIT}
Type '*1.15'	*1.15
Press 'Enter'	‾
Press Right arrow	{RIGHT}

Macros must be entered in an empty part of the spreadsheet in columnar fashion (see end of previous chapter for layout from which, however, we depart in the examples below, only because it is easier to show you what is happening).

Each command of a macro could be entered in a different row cell of that column, but since a number of commands can be combined - provided the entry is less than 240 characters long - we choose to do just that by typing in cell H10 the combined macro commands

`{EDIT}*1.15‾{RIGHT}`

and since each of the three months are to be changed, we replicate this entry using the **/Copy** command to the two rows immediately below H10.

Having thus entered the complete macro, we need to name it. To do this, highlight cell H10 and then use the **/Name Create** command. At this point you will be asked to enter the macro name which must be composed of a backslash "\" followed by a single character. In our case, we choose to call this macro \P (for percent). Thus, type

\P	to name macro
Enter	to enter name
Arrows	to highlight range of macro (in this case H10..H12)
Enter	to confirm range

It is also imperative to name your macro on the spreadsheet itself, as well as describe what it is doing. To do this, move the highlighted bar to the cell immediately to the left of the first macro entry and type "\P, so that you can remember later what you called it, then move the highlighted bar to the right of the first macro entry and describe the function of each line of the macro. This is known as the 'three-column' convention of writing macros, the structure of which is:

1st Column	2nd Column	3rd Column
Macro Name	Macro Code	Annotation

In this way, auditing macros becomes that much simpler.

Before executing any macro, save your spreadsheet, in this case under the filename MACRO1. This is a simple precaution, because should things go wrong and your macro does unpredictable things to your spreadsheet, it will be easier to reload the spreadsheet and edit the incorrect macro than it would be to also have to correct the original entries!

Your screen should now display the following information:

	B	C	D	E	F	G	H	I
1								
2								
3	Jan	Feb	Mar	1st Qrt	Average			
4	===							
5	£14,000.00	£15,000.00	£16,000.00	£45,000.00	£15,000.00			
6	===							
7								
8	2000	3000	4000	9000	£3,000.00			
9	400	500	600	1500	£500.00			
10	300	300	300	900	£300.00	\P	{EDIT}*1.15~{RIGHT}	
11	150	200	150	500	£166.67		{EDIT}*1.15~{RIGHT}	
12	250	300	350	900	£300.00		{EDIT}*1.15~{RIGHT}	
13	1100	1200	1300	3600	£1,200.00			
14	---							
15	4200	5500	6700	16400	£5,466.67			
16	===							
17	9800	9500	9300	28600	£9,533.33			
18	===							
19	9800	19300	28600					
20	===							

For easy reference, the whole of the macro is shown above, even though only part of it is visible on your screen.

To use this macro, highlight the first cell to be updated (in this case B8) and press **Alt-P**. Watch the changes that take place in cell range B8:D8 as a result of the three line macro (an empty row signifies the end of a macro), and beyond to F8, since the contents of cells E8 and F8 depend on the contents of cells B8:D8.

We could use the same macro to increase the other costs by a different percentage, by editing it, but this would be rather inefficient. A better method is to allocate a cell for the % increase, say cell H7, and edit the macro so that reference to that cell is made in absolute terms. For example, in cell G7, type

```
Incr=
```

and in cell H7 type the actual % increase (in the previous case this would have been 1.15). Finally, edit the macro to:

```
{EDIT}*$H$7~{RIGHT}
```

and copy it to the next two consecutive rows. Finally, highlight cell B8 (it is important to highlight that cell and that cell only) and press **Alt-P**. The display changes to:

	B	C	D	E	F	G	H	I	
1									
2									
3	Jan	Feb	Mar	1st Qrt	Average				
4	==								
5	£14,000.00	£15,000.00	£16,000.00	£45,000.00	£15,000.00				
6	==								
7						Incr=	1.15		
8	2300	3450	4600	10350	£3,450.00				
9	400	500	600	1500	£500.00				
10	300	300	300	900	£300.00	\P	{EDIT}*$H£7~{RIGHT}		
11	150	200	150	500	£166.67		{EDIT}*H7~{RIGHT}		
12	250	300	350	900	£300.00		{EDIT}*H7~{RIGHT}		
13	1100	1200	1300	3600	£1,200.00				
14	--								
15	4500	5950	7300	17750	£5,916.67				
16	==								
17	9500	9050	8700	27250	£9,083.33				
18	==								
19	9500	18550	27250						
20	==								

In both the last two examples, the width of column G was set to 6, so that most of the macro could be displayed on the screen at the same time as column B.

Now change the value in cell H7 to 1.20, to attempt to increase the recently increased values in B8:D8 by an additional 20%. You will notice in fact, that as soon as you change the contents of H7, the actual values in cells B8:D8 also change to reflect this new change. This, of course, will inevitably lead to errors, unless you incorporate the **/Copy Value** command within an additional macro which should be executed prior to any attempt in changing the contents of H7. Such a macro could incorporate the following commands:

```
"/CB8:D13~B8:D13,V
```

Implement this in your current spreadsheet, name it \V and save your work under the name MACRO2.

Range Names:
   It is a very good idea indeed to give range names to appropriate cells, so that reference to such cells is made by range name rather than discrete cell addressing. For example, the \V macro discussed earlier which had the commands

```
"/CB8:D13~B8:D13,V
```

could be rewritten to incorporate the range name 'Costs' as follows:

```
"/CCosts~Costs,V
```

where 'Costs' was defined as the range name for the cell block B8:D13.

   To name a block of cells by a range name, highlight the left top corner of the block and then use the **/Name Create** command, give it a name (Costs in this case) and highlight the block of cells you want to be referred to by that name (B8:D13 in this case).

   Implement this in your current spreadsheet, and save the resulting work under the name MACRO2, replacing the previously saved version. Note that we have placed both these macros (macro \P and macro \V) on specific row numbers of column H with a gap between them. This has been chosen intentionally, so as to allow room for future expansion of this example.

What you should have on your screen, is the following display:

	B	C	D	E	F	G	H	I
1								
2								
3	Jan	Feb	Mar	1st Qrt	Average			
4	==
5	£14,000.00	£15,000.00	£16,000.00	£45,000.00	£15,000.00			
6	==
7							Incr=	1.15
8	2300	3450	4600	10350	£3,450.00	\V	/CCosts~Costs,V	
9	400	500	600	1500	£500.00			
10	300	300	300	900	£300.00	\P	{EDIT}*H7~{RIGHT}	
11	150	200	150	500	£166.67		{EDIT}*H7~{RIGHT}	
12	250	300	350	900	£300.00		{EDIT}*H7~{RIGHT}	
13	1100	1200	1300	3600	£1,200.00			
14	--
15	4500	5950	7300	17750	£5,916.67			
16	==
17	9500	9050	8700	27250	£9,083.33			
18								
19	9500	18550	27250					
20	==

A final addition to the above macros could be made to allow for user entry of the 'increment' value from the keyboard, rather than having to edit cell H7. This can be achieved by the use of the GETNUMBER macro command, which allows the user to enter a number which is then inserted into the specified cell in the spreadsheet. The general format of this macro command is:

{GETNUMBER prompt-string,location}

Other available macro commands are listed in Appendix C.
In our particular case, the GETNUMBER command takes the following form:

{GETNUMBER "Incr=? ",H7}

which is typed into cell H9. Don't forget to use the **/Name Create** command to redefine macro \V to its new range, which now should be H8:H12.

Save the resulting spreadsheet under the filename MACRO3, before using it. Also, make sure that the highlighted cell is B8 before pressing the **Alt-V** keystroke. Your screen should now display the following:

	B	C	D	E	F	G	H	I
1								
2								
3	Jan	Feb	Mar	1st Qrt	Average			
4	=======	=======	=======	=======	=======			
5	£14,000.00	£15,000.00	£16,000.00	£45,000.00	£15,000.00			
6	=======	=======	=======	=======	=======			
7						Incr=	1.15	
8	2300	3450	4600	10350	£3,450.00	\V	/CCosts~Costs,V	
9	400	500	600	1500	£500.00		{GETNUMBER "Incr=? ",H7}	
10	300	300	300	900	£300.00	\P	{EDIT}*H7~{RIGHT}	
11	150	200	150	500	£166.67		{EDIT}*H7~{RIGHT}	
12	250	300	350	900	£300.00		{EDIT}*H7~{RIGHT}	
13	1100	1200	1300	3600	£1,200.00			
14					----------			
15	4500	5950	7300	17750	£5,916.67			
16					=======			
17	9500	9050	8700	27250	£9,083.33			
18					=======			
19	9500	18550	27250					
20	=======	=======	=======	=======	=======			

As a second example, use the **/Name Create** command to name the cell block A1:F20 as 'Analysis', then write a macro that will print to the printer the specified range name. Remember that to print the named range manually you would require to issue the **/Output Printer Range** command, and then press

.	(period) to anchor range from Home – cell A1
Arrows	to move cell pointer to the bottom right-hand corner of the rectangle you wish to print
Enter	to confirm selection
A	to select **Align** which resets the line counter to zero, to begin a new page
G	to select **Go** and send the report to the printer.
Q	to select **Quit**.

Implement these commands and save the resultant spreadsheet under the filename MACRO4.

Macro Keys:

Most keystrokes can be entered in a macro by typing the appropriate key. All the special macro keys must be typed as shown in the lists below. In addition all special keys (with the exception of the 'Enter' key symbol) must be enclosed in braces.

Cursor Movement Keys:

The table below lists all the cursor control keys that are allowed within macros. The 'n' in a particular macro indicates the number of times the macro is to be repeated.

Macro Key	Description
~	Enter key
{~}	Tilde appears as ~
{{} and {}}	Braces appear as { and }
{BS}	BkSp; backspace key, erases character to left of cursor. If a range is selected, erases current range
{BTAB}	Shift-Tab key; backtab prefix
{DEL}	Del; delete key, used in 'Edit' mode only
{DOWN}	Down arrow key
{END}	End key
{ENDSCR}	Ctrl-End key; move to left-right of that screen
{ESC}	Esc key; moves to next higher menu
{HOME}	Home key
{HOMESCR}	Ctrl-Home key; move to left-top of that screen
{INS}	Ins; insert key, used in 'Edit' mode only
{LEFT}	Left arrow key
{PGDN}	PgDn key
{PGLT}	Ctrl-Left arrow; move left one screen
{PGRT}	Ctrl-Right arrow; move right one screen
{PGUP}	PgUp key
{RIGHT}	Right arrow key
{TAB}	Tab key; tab prefix
{UP}	Up arrow key.

To specify two or more consecutive uses of the same key, use a repetition factor within the braces. For example,

{RIGHT 2}   causes the cell pointer to move right twice.

When a macro is created with the LEARN mode, the program uses the n method to specify command repetition.

Function Keys:

The table below lists all the function keys and their macro equivalents.

Key	Keyword	Description
F1	{HELP}	Access SuperCalc's help screen
Alt-F1	{AUDIT}	Enters AUDIT mode
F2	{EDIT}	From READY mode it calls up cell contents in entry line; from ENTRY or POINT mode it toggles on/off EDIT mode
Alt-F2	{STEP}	Toggles between normal macro execution and single-step execution
F3	{NAME}	Displays the file directory on 'Load' and 'Save' menus. In /**View** displays graph names and, in other modes, the Named Range Directory
Alt-F3	{MACRONAME}	Displays the Macro Name Directory
Ctrl-F3	{RSD}	Accesses the referenced spreadsheet directory
F4	{ABS}	In ENTRY mode it toggles the four different ways of absolute references. In the file directory, makes the current directory the default
Alt-F4	{LEARN}	Switches LEARN mode on/off
Ctrl-F4	{OSD}	Accesses the Open Spreadsheet Directory
F5	{GOTO}	Moves to a specified cell
Alt-F5	{INVOKE}	Executes a specific macro
Ctrl-F5	{GOTOSHEET}	Moves to the specified sheet
F6	{WINDOW}	Toggles between windows in a spreadsheet
Alt-F6	{DIRECT}	Switches from LEARN mode to DIRECT mode
Ctrl-F6	{SHEETWINDOW}	Toggles between spreadsheet windows
F7	{TLABELS}	Toggles between name and reference display in formulae
Ctrl-F7	{ZOOMSHEET}	Zooms in on the active sheet
F8		Resumes macro execution
Alt-F8	{RESTORE}	Switches ASTEP mode from STEP mode and restores a string removed with 'Esc'

F9	{CALC}	In ENTRY mode it solves a formula, otherwise it causes recalculation
Alt-F9	{PLOT}	Plots a chart
F10	{VIEW}	Views the currently selected chart
Ctrl-Enter	{NEWSHEET}	Opens a new sheet
Ctrl-Plus	{NEXTSHEET}	Moves to the next sheet in the cycle
Ctrl-Minus	{PREVSHEET}	Moves to the previous sheet in the cycle.

Screen control commands and logic commands for macros are given in Appendix C.

Debugging a Macro:

Writing macros can lead to mistakes which you must find and correct. To help you with this task, SuperCalc provides the STEP mode which allows you to check the execution of your macro step by step. Using this technique, you can see exactly what the macro is doing and where it is going wrong.

To invoke the STEP mode, type **Alt-F2**. The status indicator at the lower right corner of the dialogue panel will display the word STEP, and if a macro is now invoked, pressing the **F8** function key will execute it step by step, pausing after processing each of its keystrokes. Pressing **F8** again, will execute the next keystroke in the macro. If you press STEP **(Alt-F2)** again, the status indicator disappears and any macros you may invoke after that will execute normally.

If you don't want to press **F8** each time to execute the next keystroke in the macro, but you want to observe the macro execution at a comfortable speed, then press **Alt-F8** to invoke the ASTEP (auto step) mode. Pressing **Alt-F8** again, toggles back to the manual STEP mode.

There are two supporting functions to the STEP mode which are part of the menu invoked by the **//Macro** command. These are: **Trace** and **Breakpoint**. Using Trace allows you to echo the STEP mode help-line information to the printer or to a file. The **Breakpoint** option allows you to set up to eight breakpoints in a long macro so that it will automatically execute until each breakpoint is reached, when the STEP mode is invoked automatically. In this way, you don't have to step through commands that you have already debugged in step by step mode. Normal execution can be resumed again by pressing **Alt-F2** to exit the STEP mode.

Input Control with a Macro:

Finally, as an example of a macro which incorporates range names and checks the input for out of range numbers, the file MACRO3 has been added to as shown below.

	G	H	I	J	K	M	N	
6		Macro to Check Input Range						
7	Incr=	1.15			Comments:			
8	\V	{PANELOFF}			Turn panel off			
9		/CCosts~Costs,V			Copy values in range 'Costs'			
10	Strt	{PANELON}			Turn panel on			
11		{GOTO}Incr~			Go to range 'Incr'			
12		/B~			Blank range 'Incr'			
13		{GETNUMBER "Enter Value ",Incr}			Get value with prompt			
14		{IF Incr<1}{BRANCH Mstk}.			If value <1 branch to Mstk			
15		{GOTO}Costs~			Else go to range 'Costs'			
16								
17	\P	{EDIT}*H7~{RIGHT}			Multiply Contents of range			
18		{EDIT}*H7~{RIGHT}			'Costs' by contents of			
19		{EDIT}*H7~{RIGHT}			absolute location H7			
20								
21	Mstk	Error {BEEP}			Display Error, beep speaker			
22		{DELAY 3}			Delay by 2 secs			
23		{PANELOFF}			Turn panel off			
24		{BRANCH Strt}			Branch to Strt			
25								

When writing macros it is a good idea to use range names throughout. This allows you to change the location of certain portions of the macro without having to keep track of cell references and having to change such references to cell addresses. Also, a macro should be written in such a way as to anticipate any mistakes that might be made by the user. This requires a check on the input to be incorporated into it so that it provides for possible reentry of data, rather than cause abrupt exit from the particular application.

With this in mind, the above macro checks to see if an error results from a non-numeric entry, and if so, it causes the internal speaker to bleep, and asks for data reentry. If all is well, the macro causes the cursor to be placed at the beginning of the 'Costs' range so that you can choose which of the various cost categories you would like to update by activating macro \P.

Before activating this macro, it is important to turn off SuperCalc's cursor auto-advance mechanism so that no errors occur as a result of including 'Enter' (ˉ) in certain steps of the macro and then deleting the contents of the cell on which the cursor is on. To do this, use the **/Global** command, then press

−	(minus) to turn one of the toggle settings off
N	to select the **Next** option, to toggle on/off the cursor auto advance.

On completing these commands, you should notice that the arrow to the left of the spreadsheet filename on the first line of the dialogue panel has disappeared from the display.

Save the amended macro under the filename MACRO5 before running it.

*   *   *

SuperCalc5 has many more commands and functions which can be used to build and run your application in special ways. What this book has tried to do is to introduce you to the overall subject and give the beginner a solid foundation on which to build future knowledge.

APPENDIX A – MODE INDICATORS

Mode indicators are words that appear on the help line at the bottom of the screen to show which of SuperCalc's mode(s) are activated. There are three main types of indicators: Program, keyboard and macro. Within each type there are several different modes.

Program Modes:
Program mode indicators appear at the left end of the help line during every operation of SuperCalc. They inform the user of the current state or condition of the program's operation. The table below lists all the program mode indicators with their associated description.

Mode	Description
AUDIT	You have pressed **Alt-F1** or selected **//Test**. Type a single slash (/) to activate the AUDIT mode command menu which lets you locate selected types of data, find and replace formulas and text, optimize memory usage, and detect possible errors
EDIT	You have pressed **F2** or the current entry is being edited
ENTRY	You are entering data. To terminate an entry, press an **Arrow** or the **Enter** key
FILE	A menu of files is being displayed as a result of using the **/Load** or **/Save** command
INPUT	The **Restrict** command is in control. You can enter data within the restricted range
MENU	You pressed the slash key (/) and a command menu is being displayed
NAME	You pressed **F3** for the Named Range Directory of existing range names to be displayed
POINT	The highlighted bar is pointing to a cell or a range of cells
READY	The program is ready for the next command or operation
SHEET	You pressed **Ctrl-F4** to display the Open Spreadsheet Directory. Use the **Arrow** keys to select **sheetname!page**
WRAP	You have selected **/Justify Word-wrap**. While in WRAP mode, any text you type is entered in single column of the specified width.

Keyboard Modes:

Keyboard mode indicators appear at the extreme right of the help line at the bottom of the screen and inform the user of the particular condition of a key. For example, CAPS indicates that the 'Caps Lock' key is on. The table below lists all the keyboard mode indicators and gives their description.

Mode	Description
CAPS	The 'Caps Lock' key is on
END	The **End-Home** keys move the cursor to the bottom-right cell of the active spreadsheet. **End-Arrow** moves the cursor to the last occupied cell of the spreadsheet
NUM	The 'Num Lock' key is on. Enables/disables numeric keypad
SCROLL	The 'Scroll Lock' key is on. Locks the cell cursor in place and use of the **Arrow** keys, scrolls the display
TAB	Combines with the **Arrow** keys to move the cursor to the first **Tab** occupied cell.

Macro Modes:

Macro mode indicators appear on the right half of the help line (the exemption being **F8** (STEP)..., which appears on the left of the help line) when you are building or running a macro. The table below lists all the macro mode indicators together with their meaning.

Mode	Description
MACRO	A macro is executing
STEP	The macro Single-step mode is on
ASTEP	The macro Single-step mode is executing automatically
LEARN	The macro Learn mode is on
DIRECT	The macro Direct mode is on
F8 TO RESUME	Pressing **F8** terminates keyboard input and resumes macro execution
RETURN TO RESUME	Pressing 'Return' or 'Enter' terminates keyboard input and resumes macro execution
(F8)STEP L:#	Pressing **F8** single-steps through a macro with L:# being the level number in a sequence of nested macros, followed by the macro name or macro label, line number or cell and contents of the command sequence currently executing.

APPENDIX B – FUNCTIONS

SuperCalc's functions are built-in formulae that perform specialised calculations. Their general format is:

`NAME(arg1,arg2,...)`

where 'NAME' is the function name, and 'arg1', 'arg2', etc, are the arguments required for the evaluation of the function. Arguments must appear in a parenthesized list as shown above and their exact number depends on the function being used. However, there are seven functions that do not require arguments and are used without parentheses. These are: CURADDRESS, CURCOL, CURPAGE, CURROW, CURSHEET, ERR, FALSE, ITER, LASTCOL, LASTROW NA, NOW, PI, RANDOM, THISCOL, THISROW, TODAY and TRUE.

There are three types of arguments used with functions: numeric values, range values and string values, the type used being dependent on the type of function. Numeric value arguments can be entered either directly as numbers, as a cell address, a cell range name or as a formula. Range value arguments can be entered either as a range address or a range name, while string value arguments can be entered as an actual value (a string in double quotes), as a cell address, as a cell name or a formula.

Types of Functions:
There are several types of functions in SuperCalc, amongst which are mathematical, logical, financial, statistical, string, calendar, and special purpose functions. Each type requires their own number and type of arguments. These are listed below under the various function categories.

Arithmetic Functions:
Arithmetic functions evaluate a result using numeric arguments. The various functions and their meaning are as follows:

Function	Description
ABS(X)	Returns the absolute value of X
EXP(X)	Raises e to the power of X
INT(X)	Returns the integer part of X
LN(X)	Returns the natural logarithm (base e) of X
LOG(X) or LOG10(X)	Returns the logarithm (base 10) of X
MOD(X,Y)	Returns the remainder of X/Y
ROUND(X,N)	Returns the value of X rounded to N places

SQRT(X)	Returns the square root of X
TRUNC(X,N)	Returns the value of X truncated to N places.

Trigonometric Functions:

Trigonometric functions evaluate a result using numeric arguments. The various functions and their meaning are as follows:

Function	Description
ACOS(X)	Returns the angle in radians, whose cosine is X (arc cosine of X)
ASIN(X)	Returns the angle in radians, whose sine is X (arc sine of X)
ATAN(X)	Returns the angle in radians, between $\pi/2$ and $-\pi/2$, whose tangent is X (arc tangent of X − 2 quadrant)
ATAN2(X,Y)	Returns the angle in radians, between π and $-\pi$, whose tangent is Y/X (arc tangent of Y/X − 4 quadrant)
COS(X)	Returns the cosine of angle X, (X must be in radians)
PI	Returns the value of π (3.1415926)
SIN(X)	Returns the sine of angle X (X must be in radians)
TAN(X)	Returns the tangent of angle X (X must be in radians).

Logical Functions:

Logical functions produce a value based on the result of conditional statement, using numeric arguments. The various functions and their meaning are as follows:

Function	Description
AND(X,Y)	Returns 1 (TRUE) if value X and value Y are exactly alike, otherwise 0 (FALSE)
ERROR or ERR	Displays ERROR
EXACT(Sg1,Sg2)	Returns 1 (TRUE) if strings Sg1 and Sg2 are exactly alike, otherwise 0 (FALSE)
FALSE	Returns the logical value 0
IF(Cr,X,Y)	Returns the value X if Cr is TRUE and Y if Cr is FALSE
ISBLANK(X)	Returns 1 (TRUE) if X is a blank cell, else returns 0 (FALSE)

ISDATE(X)	Returns 1 (TRUE) if X is a date value cell, else returns 0 (FALSE)
ISERR(X)	Returns 1 (TRUE) if X contains ERR, else returns 0 (FALSE)
ISNA(X)	Returns 1 (TRUE) if X contains NA, else returns 0 (FALSE)
ISNUM(X)	Returns 1 (TRUE) if X contains a numeric value, else returns 0 (FALSE)
ISPROT(X)	Returns 1 (TRUE) if X is a protected cell, else returns 0 (FALSE)
ISSTR(X)	Returns 1 (TRUE) if X contains a string value, else returns 0 (FALSE)
ISTIME(X)	Returns 1 (TRUE) if cell X contains a date with value <1, else returns 0 (FALSE)
ISVAL(X)	Returns 1 (TRUE) if cell X contains a numeric value, else returns 0 (FALSE)
NA	Displays N/A for Not Available
NOT(X)	Returns 1 (TRUE) if value X is FALSE an 0 (FALSE) if value X is TRUE
OR(X,Y)	Returns 1 (TRUE) if value X or value Y are TRUE, otherwise 0 (FALSE)
TRUE	Displays 1 for logical value TRUE.

Financial Functions:

Financial functions evaluate loans, annuities, and cash flows over a period of time, using numeric arguments. The various functions and their meaning are as follows:

Function	Description
ANRATE(Pt,Pv,Tm)	Returns the periodic interest rate reflected by an annuity with an initial balance of present value Pv, paid in term Tm equal installments of payment Pt
ANTERM(Pt,Rt,Pv)	Returns the number of periods needed to reduce present value Pv to zero, at payment Pt per period for a given interest rate Rt
BALANCE(Pv,Rt, Tm,Pd)	Returns the remaining principal after period Pd payments

CTERM(Rt,Fv,Pv)	Returns the number of compounding periods for an investment of present value Pv, to grow to a future value Fv, at a fixed interest rate Rt
COMPBAL(Pv,Rt,Tm)	Returns the final balance in an account
DDB(Ct,Sg,Lf,Pd)	Returns the double-declining depreciation allowance of an asset, given the original cost Ct, predicted salvage value Sg, the life Lf of the asset, and the period Pd
FV(Pt,Rt,Tm)	Returns the future value of a series of equal payments, each of equal amount Pt, earning a periodic interest rate Rt, over a number of payment periods in term Tm
IRR(Gs,Rg)	Returns the internal rate of return of the series of cash flows in a range Rg, based on the approximate percentage guess Gs of the IRR
KINT(Pv,Rt,Tm,Pd)	Returns the amount of interest paid in the period Pd
KPRIN(Pv,Rt,Tm,Pd)	Returns the amount of principal paid in the period Pd
NPV(Rt,Rg)	Returns the present value of the series of future cash flows in range Rg, discounted at a periodic interest rate Rt
PAIDINT(Pv,Rt,Tm,Pd)	Returns the total interest paid after period Pd payments
PMT(Pv,Rt,Tm)	Returns the equal periodic payment for an ordinary annuity with an initial amount of present value Pv at interest rate Rt per period and a life of term Tm periods
PV(Pt,Rt,Tm)	Returns the present value of a series of equal payments, each of equal amount Pt, discounted at a periodic interest rate Rt, over a number of payment periods in term Tm
RATE(Fv,Pv,Tm)	Returns the periodic interest rate necessary for a present value Pv to grow to a future value Fv, over the number of compounding periods in term Tm

SLN(Ct,Sg,Lf)	Returns the straight-line depreciation allowance of an asset for one period, given the original cost Ct, predicted salvage value Sg, and the life Lf of the asset
SYD(Ct,Sg,Lf,Pd)	Returns the sum-of-the-years' digits depreciation allowance of an asset, given the original cost Ct, predicted salvage value Sg, the life Lf of the asset, and the period Pd
TERM(Pt,Rt,Fv)	Returns the number of payment periods of an investment, given the amount of each payment Pt, the periodic interest rate Rt, and the future value of the investment Fv.

Statistical Functions:

Statistical functions evaluate lists of values using numeric arguments or cell ranges. The various functions and their meaning are as follows:

Function	Description
AVG(Rg)	Returns the average of values in range Rg
COUNT(Rg)	Returns the number of non-blank entries in range Rg
MAX(Rg)	Returns the maximum value in range Rg
MIN(Rg)	Returns the minimum value in range Rg
RAND	Returns a random number between 0 and 1
STD(Rg)	Returns the standard deviation of values in range Rg
SUM(Rg)	Returns the sum of values in range Rg
VAR(Rg)	Returns the variance of values in range Rg.

String Functions:
String functions operate on strings and produce numeric or string values dependent on the function.

Function	Description
&	Concatenates strings
CHAR(X)	Returns the ASCII character that corresponds to the code number X
CODE(Sg)	Returns the ASCII code number for the first character in string Sg
CONTENTS(CI)	Returns the contents of cell CI as a string
DISPLAY(X,Ft,Wh)	Returns the string equal to value X formatted according to format string Ft and displayed at width Wh
FIND(Ss,Sg,Sn)	Returns position at which the first occurrence of search string Ss begins in string Sg, starting the search from search number Sn
LEFT(Sg,N)	Returns the first (leftmost) N characters in string Sg
LENGTH(Sg)	Returns the number of characters in string Sg
LOWER(Sg)	Returns all lower case letters in string Sg
MID(Sg,Sn,N)	Returns N characters from string Sg beginning with the character at Sn
PROPER(Sg)	Returns all words in string Sg with first letter in uppercase and the rest in lowercase
REPEAT(Sg,N)	Returns string Sg N times
REPLACE(O,S,N,Ns)	Removes N characters from original string O, starting at character S and then inserts new string Ns in the vacated place
RIGHT(Sg,N)	Returns the last (rightmost) N characters in string Sg
STRING(X,N)	Returns the numeric value X as a string, with N decimal places
TRIM(Sg)	Returns string Sg with no leading, trailing or contiguous spaces
UPPER(Sg)	Returns all letters in string Sg in uppercase.

Date and Time Functions:
Date and time functions generate and use serial numbers to represent dates and times. Each date between 1 January, 1900 and 31 December 2099 has an integer serial number starting with 1 and ending with 73050. Each moment during a day has a decimal serial number starting with 0.000 at midnight and ending with 0.99999 just before the following midnight. Thus the value 0.5 indicates midday. The various functions and their meaning are as follows:

Function	Description
DATE(Mh,Dy,Yr)	Returns the date number of the specified date
DATEVALUE(Ds)	Returns the date number of date strings Ds
DAY(Dn)	Returns the day number of date number Dn
EDAT(Dy,Mh,Yr)	Returns the European date format of the specified date
DVAL(X)	Returns the date of the specified value X
HOUR(Tn)	Returns the hour number of time number Tn
JDATE(Dn)	Returns the Julian date of date number Dn
JTIME(Tn)	Returns the Julian time of the time number Tn
MINUTE(Tn)	Returns the minute number of time number Tn
MONTH(Dn)	Returns the month number of date number Dn
NOW	Returns the serial number for the current date and time
SECOND(Tn)	Returns the second number of time number Tn
TIME(Hr,Ms,Ss)	Returns the time number of Hr,Ms,Ss
TIMEVALUE(Ts)	Returns the time number of time string Ts
TODAY	Returns the system date
TVAL(X)	Converts the fractional portion of X into time
YEAR(Dn)	Returns the year number of date number Dn
WDAY(Dn)	Returns the Julian number of the day of the week of date number Dn.

Index Functions:

Index functions perform a variety of advanced tasks, such as looking up a value in a table. The various functions and their meaning are as follows:

Function	*Description*
ADDRESS(Rg)	Returns the cell address of the upper-left cell in range Rg
BEGCOL(Rg)	Returns the column number of the upper-left cell in range Rg
BEGROW(Rg)	Returns the row number of the upper-left cell in range Rg
CHOOSE(X,V0,...,Vn)	Returns the Xth value in the list V0,..,Vn
COLS(Rg)	Returns the number of columns in the range Rg
CURADDRESS	Returns the current cell address
CURCOL	Returns the column number of the current cell
CURPAGE	Returns the number of the current spreadsheet page
CURROW	Returns the number of the current row
CURSHEET	Returns the name of the current spreadsheet
ENDCOL(Rg)	Returns the column number of the lower-right cell in range Rg
ENDROW(Rg)	Returns the row number of the lower-right cell in range Rg
HLOOKUP(X,Rg,Rn)	Performs a horizontal table look-up by comparing the value X to each cell in the top row, or index row, in range Rg, then moves down the column in which a matched is found by the specified row number Rn
INDEX(Rg,Cn,Rw)	Returns the value of the cell in range at the intersection of column Cn and row Rw
ITER	Returns the current iteration count
LASTCOL	Returns the rightmost column number containing data
LASTROW	Returns the number of the bottom row containing data
LOOKUP(X,Rg)	Returns the last value in range Rg that is less than or equal to the value X
N(CI)	Returns the numeric value of cell CI
ROW(Rg)	Returns the number of row in range Rg

S(Cl)	Returns the string value in cell Cl
VLOOKUP(X,Rg,Cn)	Performs a vertical table look-up by comparing the value X to each cell in the first column, or index column, in range Rg, then moves across the row in which a matched is found by the specified column number Cn.

Data Management Statistical Functions:

Data management statistical functions perform statistical calculations on a database. The database, which is called the input range, consists of records, which include fields and field names. A criterion range must be setup to select the records from the database that each function uses. The various functions and their meaning are as follows:

Function	Description
DAVG(Ip,Of,Cr)	Returns the average of the values in the offset column Of, of the input range Ip that meet the criteria in the criterion range Cr
DCOUNT(Ip,Os,Cr)	Returns the number of non-blank cells in the offset column Os, of the input range Ip that meet the criteria in the criterion range Cr
DMAX(Ip,Os,Cr)	Returns the maximum value in the offset column Os, of the input range Ip that meet the criteria in the criterion range Cr
DMIN(Ip,Os,CR)	Returns the minimum value in the offset column Os, of the input range Ip that meet the criteria in the criterion range Cr
DSTD(Ip,Os,Cr)	Returns the standard deviation of the values in the offset column Os, of the input range Ip that meet the criteria in the criterion range Cr
DSUM(Ip,Os,Cr)	Returns the sum of the values in the offset column Os, of the input range Ip that meet the criteria in the criterion range Cr
DVAR(Ip,Os,Cr)	Returns the variance of the values in the offset column Os, of the input range Ip that meet the criteria in the criterion range Cr.

Special-Purpose Functions:

Special-purpose functions perform a variety of advanced tasks, such as formatting values in a cell. The various functions and their meaning are as follows:

Function	Description
@(CELL)	Converts string representation of CELL into cell address
FORMAT(Cl)	Formats value of cell Cl
TYPE(Cl)	Returns character that represents cell type
VALUE(Sg)	Returns the numeric value of string Sg
WIDTH(Rg)	Returns width of column(s) where range Rg is located.

APPENDIX C – MACRO COMMANDS

There are a number of macro commands available in SuperCalc each one of which has a specified syntax. This takes one of the following two forms:

```
{Keyword}
{Keyword arg1,arg2,...,argn}
```

and must be typed into a macro with the prescribed number of arguments. Uppercase and lowercase letters are equivalent in macro keywords and are, therefore, interchangeable. However, it is a good idea to always use a different case for macro commands from that of range names. In the examples given in this book, all macro commands are entered in uppercase, while range names are entered in lowercase. This makes it easier to distinguish between the two.

Note that incorrect macro commands result in an error when the macro is invoked, and not when the macro command is entered. Also, note that there is an important difference between macros and functions. If you use the **/Move, /Insert,** and **/Delete** commands with macros, SuperCalc does not adjust specified cell addresses, therefore the macro will not work correctly. To overcome this problem, always use range names to refer to all individual cells, as well as ranges, in a spreadsheet.

SuperCalc uses two kinds of macro commands: Keyboard and programming. Keyboard macro commands automatically perform non-alphanumeric keystrokes such as **Arrow** and **Tab** keys, function keys, etc. Programming macro commands control the logic flow of the macro, data input, file input/output, and screen.

Keyboard Macros:
Following is a table of all the SuperCalc keyboard macro commands together with their corresponding keys.

Macro	Key
~	'Enter' or 'Return'
{ABS}	**F4** (toggle absolute coordinates or graphics point to current spreadsheet)
{ADD1}	through **Shift-F1** through **Shift-F10**
{ADD10}	(invokes attached add-in program)
{AUDIT}	**Alt-F1** (invokes AUDIT mode)
{BS}	BkSp (Back-Space)
{BTAB}	BkTab (Back-Tab)

87

{CALC}	**F9** (calculate spreadsheet)
{DEL}	**Del**
{DOWN}	**Down Arrow**
{EDIT}	**F2** (toggle EDIT mode)
{END}	**End**
{ENDSCR}	**Ctrl-End** (go to bottom-right cell of current window)
{ESC}	**Esc** (Escape)
{GOTO} Loc	**F5** (go to location Loc)
{GOTOSHEET} Nam	**Ctrl-F5** (go to spreadsheet Nam)
{HELP}	**F1** (display context sensitive help)
{HOME}	**Home**
{HOMESCR}	**Ctrl-Home** (go to top-left cell of current window)
{INS}	**Ins** (Insert)
{INVOKE}	**Alt-F5** or **Alt-=** (invoke macro)
{LEARN}	**Alt-F4** (toggle LEARN mode)
{LEFT}	**Left Arrow**
{MACRONAME}	**Alt-F3** (display Macro Name/Range Directory)
{NAME}	**F3** (Display Range Name Directory)
{NEWSHEET}	**Ctrl-Enter** (create new sheet)
{NEXTSHEET}	**Ctrl-Plus** (+ on the numeric keypad – go to next spreadsheet)
{OSD}	**Ctrl-F4** (display Open Spreadsheets Directory)
{PAGEDOWN}	**PgDn**
{PAGELEFT}	**Ctrl-Left Arrow**
{PAGERIGHT}	**Ctrl-Right Arrow**
{PAGEUP}	**PgUp**
{PLOT}	**Alt-F10** (plot chart)
{PREVSHEET}	**Ctrl-Minus** (- on the numeric keypad – go to previous spreadsheet)
{RIGHT}	**Right Arrow**
{RSD}	**Ctrl-F3** (display Referenced Spreadsheet Directory)
{SHEETWINDOW}	**Ctrl-F6** or **Ctrl-;** (switch spreadsheet windows)
{STEP}	**Alt-F2** (toggle Single STEP mode)
{TAB}	**Tab**
{TABLE}	**Alt-F9** (calculate table)
{TLABEL}	**F7** (names/range toggle)
{UP}	**Up Arrow**
{VIEW}	**F10** (view chart)
{WINDOW}	**F6** or **;** (switch window)
{ZOOMSHEET}	**Ctrl-F7** (display full spreadsheet from multiple spreadsheet display).

Programming Macros:
Following is a table of all the SuperCalc programming macro
commands together with their corresponding keys.

Macro	Key
{?}	Stops macro execution temporarily for keyboard input
{{}	Inserts a left-hand brace in text which is not interpreted as a macro command — there is no need for a corresponding macro statement for the closing brace
{BACKUP}	Backs up a file if it exists
{BEEP n}	Causes the speaker to bleep, with n being an optional number from 1 to 4 used for different tones (the default value is 1)
{BLANK Rg}	Erases the contents of a specified cell range Rg
{BLANKC Rg}	Performs the same function as **/Blank Contents,** blanking only contents of the specified range, not entry level formats
{BRANCH Loc}	Causes macro execution to branch to a different location
{BREAKOFF}	Disables the BREAK key during macro execution
{BREAKON}	Enables normal BREAK key function
{CLOSE}	Closes a file that has been opened with the OPEN command
{COMMENT Sg}	Places comments in a macro
{DEFINE Cl1,..,Cl32}	Enters {CALL} arguments into specified cells
{DELAY n}	Delays the processing of the macro for the number of seconds specified by n
{DISPATCH Loc}	Branches indirectly to the specified destination, given by Loc
{ENTRYOFF}	Clears the entry line
{ENTRYON}	Restores normal display and operation of the entry line
{ERRMSG Sg}	Displays a user defined error message specified by "Sg"
{FILESIZE Loc}	Determines the number of bytes in a currently opened file and places it in specified Location

{FOR Count,Start, Stop,Step,Startloc}	Executes repeatedly the macro subroutine that begins at the Start location. Count is a cell in which SuperCalc holds the current number of repetition, while Startloc is the first cell, or range name of which subroutine to be executed
{FORBREAK}	Cancels execution of FOR loop
{GET Loc}	Stops macro execution temporarily and stores a single character you type in a specified cell given by Loc
{GETCELLS Prmt,Loc}	Stops macro execution temporarily, and prompts you with "Prmt" to enter a cell or a cell range to store as text in the specified location given by Loc
{GETCOLS Prmt,Loc}	Stops macro execution temporarily, and prompts you with "Prmt" to enter a column letter or a column range to store as text in the specified location given by Loc
{GETKEY Prmt,Loc}	Stops macro execution temporarily, and prompts you with "Prmt" to press a key, and stores the key in the specified location given by Loc
{GETNUMBER Prmt,Loc}	Stops macro execution temporarily, and prompts you with "Prmt" to type a numeric value into the specified cell given by Loc
{GETPOS Loc}	Determines the current position of the file pointer in an open file and displays it in Loc
{GETROWS Prmt,Loc}	Stops macro execution temporarily, and prompts you with "Prmt" to enter a row number or a row range to store as text in the specified location given by Loc
{GETTEXT Prmt,Loc}	Stops macro execution temporarily, and prompts you with "Prmt" to enter text and stores the text in the specified location given by Loc
{GOCURRENT}	Returns macro execution to the spreadsheet and page that was current before {GOMACRO} was executed
{GOMACRO}	Makes the macro spreadsheet the current spreadsheet, causing the macro to execute in the macro spreadsheet

{IF Condition}	Conditionally executes the succeeding command
{INDICATOR String}	Changes the program mode indicator of the help line
{INSERTOFF}	Turns the Insert mode off
{INSERTON}	Turns the Insert mode on
{KEY}	Interrupts macro execution and awaits for a key press, which executes as part of the macro
{LABEL Ll}	Names a label in a file macro which can be referenced by {BRANCH}, {MENU}, {CALL}, and so on
{LET Loc,Exp}	Stores an entered expression in a specified cell given by Loc
{LETC Loc Frm}	Puts formula "Frm" into location Loc, as if it was entered from the entry line
{LOOK Loc}	Scans the keyboard for input during macro execution and stores that character in Loc
{MACROPROMPT Sg}	Controls the macro prompt area of the help line that normally displays the macro modes and prompts
{MENU Loc}	Indicates the beginning of a menu
{MESSAGE Sg}	Controls the appearance of the help message area of the help line
{ONBREAK Loc}	Directs macro execution to location Loc upon **Ctrl-Break**
{ONERROR Rt,Msg,Loc}	Sets up an interrupt handler for errors that would normally abort a macro. When an error occurs, macro control transfers to the specified routine Rt
{OPEN Filename, Mode}	Opens the specified file in the current directory for reading or writing. Mode is a single character (R for Reading, W for Write or M for Modify) which describes the type of file access
{OVERWRITE}	Overwrites a file if it exists
{PANELOFF}	Disables redrawing of control panel during macro execution
{PANELON}	Enables control panel redrawing
{PROMPT Sg}	Controls the entire prompt line, characters 1 to 80
{QUIT}	Terminates macro execution and returns control to the keyboard

{READ Bytes,Loc}	Reads a number of bytes (characters) from a file into a cell specified by Loc
{READLN Loc}	Copies a line of characters from the currently open file into the specified location
{READY}	Returns to the READY mode
{RECALC Rg,Con,ltn}	Recalculates the formulae in the specified range Rg, row by row. Con is optional argument; It is evaluated after the range is calculated and if Con is FALSE, it calculates the range again; ltn specifies the number of times the range is calculated
{RECALCCOL Rg,Con,ltn}	Recalculates the formulae in a specified range, column by column under the same conditions as RECALC
{REPLACE}	Forces a Zap of the current spreadsheet before loading or importing another spreadsheet from disc
{RESTART}	Cancels the subroutine and clears the subroutine stack
{RETURN}	Returns from a subroutine
{SETPOS Ptr Pos}	Sets the file Pointer in the currently opened file into the new position specified by Pos
{STATUS Sg}	Controls the entire status line, character 1 to 80
{SUSPEND}	Stops macro execution temporarily and allows keyboard entry until F8 is pressed
{WINDOWSOFF}	Disables redrawing the display screen during macro execution
{WINDOWSON}	Enables normal screen redrawing
{WRITE Sg}	Copies characters given by Sg into an open file, at the current pointer position
{WRITELN Sg}	Adds a carriage-return line-feed sequence to a string of characters given by Sg and writes the string to a file at the current pointer position.

INDEX

Notes.

Notes.